How to Pass Your EXAMS

Visit our How To website at <u>www.howto.co.uk</u>

At <u>www.howto.co.uk</u> you can engage in conversation with our authors – all of whom have 'been there and done that' in their specialist fields. You can get access to special offers and additional content but most importantly you will be able to engage with, and become a part of, a wide and growing community of people just like yourself.

At <u>www.howto.co.uk</u> you'll be able to talk and share tips with people who have similar interests and are facing similar challenges in their lives. People who, just like you, have the desire to change their lives for the better – be it through moving to a new country, starting a new business, growing your own vegetables, or writing a novel.

At <u>www.howto.co.uk</u> you'll find the support and encouragement you need to help make your aspirations a reality.

For more information on passing exams visit <u>www.passyourexams.co.uk</u>

How To Books strives to present authentic, inspiring, practical information in their books. Now, when you buy a title from **How To Books,** you get even more than just words on a page.

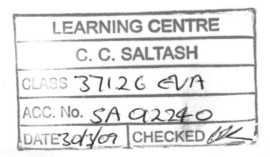

How to Pass Your EXAMS

Proven techniques for any exam
that will boost your confidence
and guarantee success

THIRD EDITION · THIRD EDITION ·

MIKE EVANS

howtobooks

Published by How To Books Ltd,
Spring Hill House, Spring Hill Road,
Begbroke, Oxford OX5 1RX
Tel: (01865) 375794. Fax: (01865) 379162
info@howtobooks.co.uk
www.howtobooks.co.uk

Second edition 2004
Reprinted 2005
Reprinted 2006
Third edition 2009

ISBN 978-1-84528 323 0

British Library Cataloguing in Publication Data
A catalogue record for this book is available from the British Library

Produced for How To Books by Deer Park Productions, Tavistock
Typeset by PDQ Typesetting, Newcastle-under-Lyme, Staffs.
Printed and bound in Great Britain by Bell & Bain Ltd, Glasgow

Contents

Preface

Compared with the nine months or so of hard work involved in undertaking a course of study and submitting coursework assignments, exams themselves actually *are* easy. Yet it's the exams that people dread more than anything else. This is partly because students are generally not taught how to approach exams in a way that builds the necessary confidence and maximises their chances. In this book I'll help take the fear out of exams and give you some practical tips on how to do well in them.

Exam success isn't only for the clever and hard working. Success comes as much, if not more, from your attitude to exams, the way you approach the course of study and some simple techniques to use on the day itself.

A universal culture of fear, worry and stress has developed around exams. But it really needn't be like this for you. In this book I will dispel the common myths surrounding exams and show you how to adopt a positive and confident approach. Some simple insights, tools and approaches are provided which are rarely taught in schools and colleges, but which can really make the difference between success and failure. In fact they are likely to account for at least 50% of your chances for success.

We'll start by getting you to change completely the way you view exams. Next we move on to looking at what examiners want from you. And then, armed with the attitude and confidence to do well, you'll see how to study and revise in a way that minimises the pressure at exam time whilst at the same time equipping you to succeed. Finally, you'll learn some simple but absolutely invaluable tips on how to approach the exam itself. The techniques are easy to learn and proven beyond doubt and have the added advantage of giving your confidence a welcome boost, so that you arrive in the exam room ready and able to succeed.

Your chance of success will improve dramatically and you will gain an immediate advantage over the not-so-enlightened; an advantage from changing your *attitude, thinking and technique* throughout your course of study and, most importantly, on the day of the exam; an advantage gained through building confidence, the all-too-often missing ingredient which can reduce intelligent, capable people to nervous wrecks at exam time!

Mike Evans

Getting a Sensible Perspective

In this chapter you'll learn how to view exams in a completely different light. We'll sweep away all the myths and misconceptions and examine the common causes of failure. Finally, you'll see how to develop a positive attitude and take responsibility for your own success.

CHANGE YOUR THINKING

Before we can move on to the practicalities of doing well in exams you need to understand that one of the greatest barriers to success is your *attitude* to the whole exam process. As with many things in life the way you *choose* to view this can change your feelings and performance dramatically.

I'm going to show you that the common fears relating to exams are completely unfounded leaving you free to choose, with some justification, to view examinations not as threatening but more as an opportunity to demonstrate your knowledge and skills and to do well. We'll also talk about stress and how to avoid the harmful effects whilst harnessing the positive effects.

Understanding the things that usually go wrong is a key element of changing your thinking. By seeing how easy it is to avoid these pitfalls you'll begin to feel much more confident and able to face exams without fear.

You'll also see how to improve your chances dramatically by taking responsibility yourself for your own success rather than relying too heavily on teachers, lecturers, etc.

DISPEL THE COMMON FEARS AND MYTHS – NOW!

Fears and myths relating to exams can reach almost hysterical proportions in some cases. And from an early age we learn to dread exams and view them as a necessary evil. The most common fears are:

♦ Exam questions are carefully worded to catch you out.

♦ Examiners are very mean with marks.

♦ Exams are nothing more than a test of memory, so they favour those with perfect recall or a photographic memory.

♦ You can only do well in exams if you can think and write quickly.

♦ You're bound to get stressed by exams and this can be very dangerous and destructive.

None of this is true. Let me explain...

Exams are not designed to catch you out

Exams aim to test your *understanding* in a constructive way. Questions need to be worded very carefully to:

- ◆ Minimise or eliminate any potential misunderstandings.

- ◆ Ensure that everyone has the same chance of understanding and answering them correctly to make the marking process fair.

> What is usually misinterpreted as too exacting is nothing more than an honest attempt at clarity!

Examiners are required to write questions in a manner which gives you the opportunity to demonstrate your abilities rather than exposing any weaknesses. Examining boards and authorities exist to *promote* knowledge and understanding, not to discourage achievement.

But, and it's a very big **BUT**, having worded the question very carefully they do expect you to do *exactly* what they've asked and present your answer in a clear, logical and easy-to-read way. We'll talk more about this later, *ad nauseam*, because you'll see it come up time and time again. I make no apology for this because one of the biggest causes of failure is not answering the question properly.

Examiners are very nice people

Well maybe some aren't, but they're certainly not mean with marks and they take no pleasure in failing people. They are usually from the teaching profession so they understand and sympathise with students. For internally-set exams they are often your own lecturers or teachers and in those cases your failure could reflect badly on them. I'm certainly not suggesting that they would award a pass where it isn't justified, but they're certainly on your side and have no interest at all in catching you out unfairly.

Examiners want you to pass. And they like awarding marks – providing you've done what was asked. They have a carefully designed marking scheme for each carefully worded question so they want to allocate the marks in accordance with this. This means that in reality the marking process usually consists of the examiner *searching* your answer for responses or points which will earn marks. So as soon he finds one he will allocate the marks and look for the next award-earning item.

Bear in mind also that he is usually faced with marking hundreds of scripts to a very tight deadline, so he wants to get through them as quickly and effectively as possible. There is a very important, fundamental fact to be highlighted here. You can capitalise on this situation by *making it easy for the examiner to award marks*, i.e. get him on your side from the outset. How can you do this? It's simple:

- Make sure you answer the question by doing exactly what is asked.

- Make your answer easy to read by presenting it in a logical, easy-to-follow manner with the key points brought out clearly. This makes it easy for the examiner to award the marks as well as keeping him in a good mood.

We'll cover both of these points in Chapter 2. You'll see how to read and interpret questions as well as how to present an easy-to-read response.

Exams are not tests of memory
Exams are designed to test your understanding of and ability to apply the course concepts. This obviously requires you to remember

a degree of detail but that's not what you're being tested on.

We'll be discussing later how best to study and organise your course materials (see Chapter 3) as well as effective revision techniques (see Chapter 5). All of this will help consolidate your learning so that you'll find your memory will be good enough. Students invariably have moments of panic about memory close to exams but then they find that the exam questions prompt sufficient recall as they begin to focus on the answer. The irony here is that students usually remember too much and consequently try to write it all down when the question doesn't actually require it.

Knowing what to leave out is a more common problem
than remembering enough to put in.

We'll be discussing this more when we look at planning answers in Chapter 6.

Exams are not tests of writing speed

Exams are designed to be capable of completion in the allotted time. The perception that there's never enough time comes back to what I've said above – students try to write all they know about a subject rather than concentrate specifically on what is asked. But you'll never be asked to 'write all you know' about a topic, so don't ever think about doing it.

We're back to the common mistakes of not reading the question carefully and not planning a concise, clearly focussed answer to which the examiner can allocate marks easily. By the time you've finished this book you'll see how to avoid these problems.

Of course you have to work quickly in an examination, but there is enough time to finish, and furthermore it's vital that you attempt the required number of questions. I'll demonstrate later on that there is actually no excuse for not finishing provided you manage your time carefully. (See Chapter 8.)

You don't need to get too stressed by exams

A degree of stress helps bring out the best in most people. People often perform better under some pressure so the trick is to harness the positive effects of stress whilst minimising the more negative aspects.

How you achieve this will depend very much on the type of individual you are. In this book I hope to take away some of the negative aspects by:

◆ Dispelling the myths associated with exams.
◆ Eliminating the irrational fears.
◆ Changing your attitude.
◆ Improving your study and revision technique.
◆ Improving your exam technique.

Thereby leaving you with a healthy level of stress sufficient to bring out the best in you.

It can be a complicated area because stress and anxiety affect people in many different ways. This book will alleviate the effects for everyone and hopefully eliminate them for many. But if problems persist then look for other sources of help which, incidentally, will help in many aspects of your life, not just exams, so the effort is likely to be very worthwhile. There is a wealth of literature available nowadays on stress management covering such things as:

◆ Exercise
◆ Diet
◆ Relaxation techniques
◆ Natural therapies
◆ Positive thinking, etc.

If you haven't already done so, you may find it useful to try some of these.

For my part, I ask that you view stress as a two edged sword as far as exams are concerned.

> Look for the positive side. See exams as an opportunity
> to do well and achieve more than you might otherwise.

Use this book to:

◆ Improve your understanding of what examiners require.
◆ Build your confidence.
◆ Get rid of some of the misconceptions and myths.

Many argue that the exam system puts terrible stress on young people and this sometimes has tragic consequences. Such stress is more often than not founded on irrationality and those who experience extreme symptoms should seek medical help immediately. Life puts many stresses on the young and learning to cope with exams can help them in later life. Many learn to thrive on stress through seeing the various challenges as opportunities to do well.

THE THINGS THAT USUALLY GO WRONG

If you don't do much work throughout the course and you do little or no revision then you'll probably fail, and you deserve to. There are no magic answers for the student who does hardly any work. But many failures arise even where very capable people have studied very hard. Such instances can seem curious or even bordering on the mysterious. After all, if someone is clever and they do all the work then they are bound to pass, aren't they? Sadly no! They can fail for any of a number of reasons not related to the actual volume of effort expended in their studies or their innate academic abilities.

Let's look at these, but first let me say that all these problems can be avoided easily. I'll show you how in later chapters. For now all you need is a general awareness of the sort of things that can and do go wrong regularly for even the most conscientious students.

Relying solely on the tutor/lecturer to teach them everything

Relying solely on your tutor to equip you with everything you need for success is a dangerous strategy. How often have you heard candidates leaving an exam room saying '...we didn't cover half the stuff that came up...'.

The day of the exam is one heck of a time to discover that you've not covered everything you needed to.

Later in this chapter I'll be talking more about this and how you must start taking responsibility for your own success. For now just hold on to the idea *that the best person to look out for your interests is you.*

Poorly planned and ineffective revision

There are much easier, more effective and enjoyable ways to revise than a marathon cramming exercise in the weeks leading up to the exam with a very late session on the last night. These are explained in Chapter 5.

Poor note keeping which makes revision confusing, difficult and time consuming

You'll see in Chapter 3 how to get organised from the beginning of the course, including how to use notes effectively and thereby minimising the effort required for revision.

Failure to read questions properly

Here's where things start to go wrong in the exam room, but in Chapters 2 and 8 I'll give you some techniques to avoid this common mistake.

Poor essay technique and failing to plan answers properly

Another big problem area where people fail to grasp the importance of *the way in which they communicate with the examiner*. Remember what I said earlier about making it easy for the examiner to give you marks? In Chapter 6 you'll learn all about planning and writing essays to achieve this.

Failure to manage time effectively during the exam

We've already talked about the need to plan your time to finish the exam. In Chapter 8 you'll see exactly how to do this. Remember *there's no excuse for not finishing!*

Recognising the importance of the common mistakes

The important thing to note about all of the points above is that they *are nothing to do with the content of the course itself.* They are common to all exams and the solutions require very little investment of your time to master the appropriate techniques. A few hours spent reading this book will stand you in good stead for examinations of all types. The approach is relevant to virtually any type of exam whether professional or academic, masters level or GCSE, essay or multiple choice.

These techniques and approaches count for at least 50% of your chances for success, yet they represent a relatively minimal amount of your investment in terms of time. So it's a pretty good deal isn't it? Accept this and you're well on the way to making this book really work for you.

I have known cases where students didn't do enough work but actually achieved a pass through effective use of these techniques. In fact this has happened to me on more than one occasion. I'm certainly not suggesting that you try to get by with as little work as possible – that's far too risky, but I am emphasising the importance of what you are about to learn.

The techniques are proven beyond doubt as well as being easy to understand and apply effectively.

The benefits have been enjoyed by many over the years including myself, my students, colleagues, friends and my own children.

DEVELOPING A POSITIVE ATTITUDE AND TAKING RESPONSIBILITY FOR YOUR OWN SUCCESS

I hope that you can now begin to see that you needn't worry about exams quite so much. By the time you've finished the book I hope you'll be convinced that the exams themselves are the least of your worries. The hard bit is working through the course and understanding the concepts and ideas. *The exams are the easy bit!* By the time you enter the exam room the worst is over and, armed with these newly-found techniques, you might even find you enjoy them. That's not as daft as it may first sound, because students who come out of an exam feeling they have coped well do experience an amazing sensation of well-being.

The grand conspiracy in your favour

If you're still feeling that the whole exam process is a conspiracy to make things difficult, let's work on eliminating those negative thoughts. We've established already that:

◆ Exams are not designed to catch you out.

◆ They provide an opportunity for you to demonstrate your abilities.

◆ Examiners like giving marks to people who do what is asked of them.

◆ Exams can be completed in the allotted time.

◆ Everyone's memory is sufficient.

Add to this the fact that you have probably *chosen* to undertake the course and you almost certainly wouldn't be doing it if you haven't got what it takes. Think also about the positive outcomes when you succeed.

So, obviously, you want to pass, the examiners want you to pass (believe me they do!), your tutors want you to pass and I'm sure your family and friends want you to pass. That's a lot of positive vibes before you even start. In fact there appears to be a grand conspiracy in your favour going on here.

So don't let a few negative, irrational thoughts spoil it.

I'll also be highlighting the various sources of help available which few take advantage of. Students who cocoon themselves in an isolated state of helplessness are making things unnecessarily difficult. There's a lot of help around, all you have to do is make a little effort to secure it.

And don't even begin to think that luck plays a major part. There will always be some elements of the course that you feel more comfortable with than others, and you will no doubt feel lucky if questions come up on those. But in the grand scheme of things this isn't a make-or-break factor in exam success.

By the time you've read this book you'll be feeling confident in your approach, leaving any thoughts of luck to your chances in the national lottery.

Taking responsibility for your own success

You've already started to take responsibility for your own success by reading this book. What I have to say isn't earth shattering or revolutionary. I hope you'll see it more as good sense. But it isn't usually taught in schools and colleges (which to me is bizarre, given that it accounts for at least 50% of your chances) yet takes only a tiny percentage of time to learn relative to the course content.

I'll show you how to take control of the whole learning process right from the start, through your revision and in the exam itself.

The problem of finding out in the exam room that you've not covered the syllabus is a good example where taking responsibility for your own success is vital. Tutors, teachers and lecturers are no different to members of any other profession or trade. They're not infallible and there are good ones and bad ones. Time constraints often mean that they deliberately exclude certain elements of the course. This may be appropriate if the exams typically provide sufficient choice for this not to be a problem. But this may be a very risky approach – risky for you that is, not the tutor. And being able to blame him is absolutely no consolation; it's all too late.

So why entrust your future completely to someone else when there are a few simple things you can do to avoid getting caught out like this? These relate to getting hold of a copy of the syllabus and monitoring your progress against it. We'll talk more about this in Chapter 3.

I once knew an A-level economics student at a comprehensive school who was experiencing problems with the course due to poor quality teaching arising from staff turnover, sickness etc. It was a good school and he was used to being 'spoon-fed' but in desperation he decided to study economics himself, in his own time and directly from recommended textbooks. He also got hold of as many past papers as possible and practised answering them. Having initially felt very disgruntled at having to do this he then began to get quite a buzz through achieving a high level of understanding from his own efforts.

He achieved a high grade and went on to study economics at university where he gained a first class honours degree.

There was a useful by-product of all this. His experience at A-level equipped him very well for university where students are expected to research and learn things themselves. He noted that some of his fellow students who had experienced excellent teaching at A-level, found the change to more self-managed learning to be quite a struggle.

Nowadays, education and personal development operates much more on a basis of individuals taking responsibility for their own learning. So the earlier you accept this fact the easier you'll find things in the long run.

And finally. . .

That's the end of the pep talk (for now at least) and in the next few chapters we'll turn to the more practical matters which will help justify the optimism you should now be feeling. Remember, though, the need to stay positive and recognise that with the right mental attitude, the correct approach to your studies and some easy-to-learn techniques you really can *pass exams every time.*

CHECKLIST

✓   Remember that no one is trying to catch you out. Careful
    reading of a carefully framed question provides the
    opportunity for you to do well.

✓   The common causes of failure are easy to avoid. Make sure
    you understand them.

✓   Recognise the positive aspects of stress and find out how
    to minimise the negative effects.

✓   Recognise and take advantage of the fact that everyone,
    including the examiner, wants you to pass.

✓   Start taking responsibility for your own success – right
    now!

2

What Examiners Want

In this chapter we'll look at what examiners want you to do. They're the ones in position to award marks (and remember — they like doing that!) but they can only do that if you produce what's needed. Unfortunately, students often fail to understand what is actually needed. This applies equally both to *what* the answer should contain and *how* it's presented. What's even more tragic is that many of these students have worked very hard on revision and could have avoided failure by following a few simple rules on how to give the examiner what he wants.

SOME MORE MYTHS AND MISCONCEPTIONS

The whole exam process is surrounded by myths, misconceptions and fears and this applies as much to what people think examiners want as to anything else. The common misapprehensions include:

♦ 'If I bombard the examiner with enough facts he'll see I've done the work and is bound to grant me a pass.'

♦ 'Exams are not about essay writing skills, they're just about showing the examiner you know the facts.'

♦ 'There's not enough time in an exam to worry about how you present things, so I just concentrate on getting the facts down.'

- 'I have very strong political and moral views on most things and I always try to get these across in an exam.'

Sounds familiar? Well, before we move on from the myths to the reality, let's start with a couple of reminders from Chapter 1:

- Exams aim to *test your understanding* in a constructive way.

- Examiners are required to write questions in a way which gives you the opportunity to demonstrate your abilities, not to show how good your memory is.

- Examining boards and authorities exist to *promote* knowledge and understanding, not to discourage achievement.

Examiners' reports

Many examining boards ask their examiners to produce reports each year which explain the general performance of candidates. The same concerns are highlighted year-in-year-out. They invariably read something like this:

- 'Many students did not read the instructions at the head of the question paper. Some answered fewer than required and some even answered more! Some failed to answer the required number from each section and others missed out elements of a multi-part question.'

- 'Students did not read the questions carefully enough. A question in a 20th century history paper asking for causes of the outbreak of World War 1 prompted answers from some candidates relating to World War 2!'

- 'Students did not take careful note of the verb in the question which told them what to do e.g. *assess, compare, describe, argue, list*, etc. Instead they regurgitated all they could think of about the topic involved.'

- 'Students did not plan their answers. They produced an uncoordinated mass of prose which jumped around from point to point with no logical thread running through the answer. In short, there was no structure or logic to the answer which made it very difficult to mark.'

- 'Judgements and viewpoints were not supported by clear evidence. Lack of objectivity was often evident with wild generalisations and personal prejudices included.'

- 'Students did not manage their time effectively which meant that many did not finish. Others wrote unnecessarily long answers to some questions and only a few lines for the final ones because they ran out of time.'

All too familiar unfortunately, and tragic that some students who have worked very hard and revised thoroughly will fail or get a lower grade because of the *way* they approach the exam on the day. But it's very easy to avoid these mistakes and I'm going to show you how.

SO WHAT DO THEY WANT?

It's very important to understand the process from the examiners' viewpoint. They're the people with the marks to give and you need to know what will earn those marks for you. So learn how to keep them on your side from the start. And don't think that regurgitating facts is all that's required, there's much more to it than that, as you'll see.

They want you to pass

I hope that I convinced you of this in Chapter 1 but it's worth mentioning again. Remember also that the marking process is all about awarding marks so you need to know how to take advantage of this. This has to be good news but remember there are a few strings attached. They expect you to do exactly what is asked and present your answer in a clear, logical and easy-to-read way. The examiners' reports referred to above show this clearly.

They want you to do what is asked

You stand little or no chance of doing what's required unless you:

◆ Read the *instructions* on the question paper carefully.

◆ Read each *question* carefully.

This is where the serious problems usually begin. In a heightened state of anxiety, a student is very keen to begin writing, especially if the candidate sitting next to them has already started within about ten seconds of turning the paper over. That person is well on the way to failure and you'll understand why by the time you've finished this book. It's vital that you spend a little time reading both the instructions and each question carefully. We'll be discussing this in more detail in Chapter 8. For now, though, I'd like you to appreciate the importance of getting a clear understanding of what you are required to do.

They want you to follow the instructions

It is vital to ensure that you know:

◆ How many questions to answer.

- Whether any are compulsory.

- If the question paper is divided into sections, how many you must answer from each section.

They want you to answer the question

Remember, you will not be asked to *'Write all you know about...'* . The examiner is not interested in whether you can memorise facts and simply repeat them. So it's important to ascertain exactly what is being asked. Below is a selection (not an exhaustive list) of the type of *verbs* used typically in essay questions and (my suggestions of) what they mean.

Account for	Explain why something is so.
Analyse	Explain the main points in detail.
Argue	Make a case for and/or against a particular viewpoint and back it up with objective evidence.
Assess	Using your knowledge of the course and associated issues, judge the degree to which something is so.
Compare	Identify similar characteristics and differences between two or more things.
Contrast	Point out differences between (and possibly, briefly acknowledge similarities).
Criticise	Judge something showing its shortcomings backed with logical argument to support your criticism.

- **Describe**   Give a detailed account.

- **Discuss**   Examine the case for and against.

- **Explain**   Show clearly why something is so.

- **Identify**   Pick out key features.

- **Illustrate**   Explain something with examples.

- **Justify**   Show reasons for something.

- **List**   Compile a list.

- **Prove**   Demonstrate, with evidence, why something is so.

- **Review**   Survey and make an assessment of something.

- **Summarise**   State the main points.

- **Trace**   Show the development of the history of something, explaining the various stages.

- **Verify**   Show why something is true.

Look for the verb!
And think carefully about what it means.

You will be judged critically against how well you respond to it. The common mistake is to look for the subject matter and write all you know about it. Of course the subject matter is important, but what you do with it and how you present it will earn you the marks.

They want you to apply the course concepts

The reason these verbs are so important comes back to the whole point of exams, which is to test your *understanding* of the course concepts and your ability to *apply* them. The examiner will have chosen her words carefully to test you in a particular way so it's vital that you look very carefully at what is required. By now I'm sure you can see that being asked to 'Argue', 'Compare', 'Discuss' or 'Justify' is different from regurgitating loads of facts. You must be able to select the appropriate material to include in your answer and, just as importantly, know what to leave out.

They want you to use logical and coherent arguments

They want you to draw on the course content and apply it sensibly and objectively. Wild generalisations, personal anecdotes and your own political or moral preferences just will not do. I once studied with a very clever chap (an Oxford graduate) who repeatedly failed an economics paper in a professional examination. This surprised everyone and he was in serious danger of being unable to qualify in his chosen field. In conversation one day he happened to say, 'I have very strong political views and I always make sure I get these across in the exam'. It was pointed out to him that this was likely to be the reason for his repeated failures and he passed at the next attempt.

Where it's difficult to come to a clear view you can say that the arguments are inconclusive or that there are merits on either side, dependent on circumstances. What you must be able to show is that you have understood the key arguments on each side – that's what will earn you the marks. If you are asked specifically to express an opinion then ensure it's supported by logical argument.

> The examiner is looking for an objective analysis and
> reasoned arguments based on your understanding
> of the course content and associated ideas.

View the exam as an opportunity to show that you have understood the course. Bring in the course ideas and back them up with evidence. For example, if you wish to make the point that traditional village life is threatened by wealthy city workers buying and renovating country properties then it must be more than simply your opinion or just hearsay. You would need to substantiate this by reference to official sociological research and evidence on house prices.

They want you to structure and present your answer in a way that's easy to follow

Having read the question carefully and identified the key verb(s) you need to think about how you will tackle your answer. You'll be starting to think of the main points and these will generate further thoughts and you'll be anxious to get these down on paper.

But you need to pause briefly and think about how you can capture these thoughts, ideas and facts in a way that ensures you will produce a clear, logical and well-structured answer. By all means get your thoughts down on paper but starting to write your answer immediately isn't the best way. Jot them down in the form of a plan. This will help you to collect your thoughts and sort your ideas into a logical sequence. You can then structure your answer sensibly and stick to the point as you write your answer.

You cannot write a good essay without planning it first.
Examiners like to see essay plans.

The plan will enable you to write an essay comprising an introduction, main body and conclusion, all split into paragraphs with concise sentences and a direct style of writing. This will make it easy for the examiner to follow and to award marks. In the unlikely event that you run out of time, then the examiner can see from your plan what you were intending to say.

And they don't want the question written out at the beginning of your answer, so don't waste time doing this.

One of my students used to write out each question in red ink, underline it three times in green ink and draw a blue box around the whole thing – a complete waste of time.

We'll talk in more detail about planning and writing essays in Chapter 6.

They want the answers to be legible

There's nothing to be ashamed of if your handwriting isn't the best. Nowadays people are becoming much less used to writing large quantities, preferring instead to use word processors. But think of the examiner. If it's difficult for him to read your script then he's unlikely to feel over-charitable about awarding marks. Handwriting also suffers as panic sets in – so don't let it!

All I can suggest if your writing is difficult to read is that you practise making it a little clearer. If you combine this with a really well laid out answer in terms of paragraph and sentence construction, then I'm sure you'll be OK. Examiners are used to dealing with poor handwriting because answers are written quickly. But you need to be aware of the difference between poor and illegible.

They want you to finish the paper
The examination paper is put together very carefully and sufficient time is allowed to complete it.

◆ The intention is that you should complete it

and furthermore...

◆ you are *instructed* to answer a specific number of questions.

Students who mismanage their time tend to produce a very long first answer, a shorter (but still too long) second answer and ever-shortening subsequent answers as time begins to run out. So the last one or two are either omitted altogether or comprise just a few notes.

This is a sure-fire way of losing marks.

They've probably done more than they need on the early questions and gained no extra marks and eliminated or reduced the chances of getting acceptable marks on the later questions.

Some students deliberately adopt a strategy of
answering fewer questions but doing them 'really well'.
This is seriously flawed – don't do it.

Not only will you have ignored the carefully considered instructions, but you are also reducing seriously your chances of success. We'll come back to this in Chapter 8 when we talk about managing your time.

CHECKLIST

✓ Think about what the examiner wants – he's the person in a position to award the marks you need.

✓ Get into the habit of reading very carefully the instructions at the beginning of each exam paper. Start this *now* with any past papers you read or practise.

✓ Read questions very carefully. Highlight the key verb(s) and think carefully about what they mean. Again, start this *now* with any past papers you read or practise.

✓ Think about applying course concepts and ideas to your answers. Construct logical answers with well-supported arguments. Start this now for any coursework or practice papers – it doesn't just apply to the real exam.

✓ Plan your answers before you start to write them. Think about the structure and paragraphs.

✓ Practise writing legibly at speed.

✓ Think about planning and managing your time so that you finish the exam and have a good crack at all the marks available.

We'll be dealing with all the above again later in the book and you'll learn how to apply these ideas easily and effectively. But it's important to get them planted firmly in your mind right from the outset.

$$\binom{3}{}$$

Getting Set for Success

Now we move on to some of the practicalities. In this chapter you'll see how to get yourself organised in such a way as to minimise the final revision workload. As well as planning your time and organising your course materials, it also involves thinking about the exams right from the outset of the course. You may not like the sound of this initially; but stick with it and you'll see how you can make life much easier overall and feel more confident as a result.

TAKE THE HEAT OUT OF THE EXAMS

You can do a lot to make your exams easy by getting organised from the outset of the course. In this chapter we'll talk about some of the practicalities for studying in a way that eases the final revision, as well as introducing some fresh approaches regarding how you work throughout the academic year.

Finding time to study and prepare for exams is a challenge for virtually every student. If you're a parent with a full-time job and studying by distance learning you will experience many conflicting pressures and far too many demands on your time. Even full-time students at school or college will find that they have too much to do. Coursework, youth activities such as the Duke of Edinburgh Award scheme, part-time jobs, holidays and a social life all conspire to fill your time. As deadlines approach, feelings of pressure and anxiety mount and it can all get a bit overwhelming.

And I'm afraid it may appear at first that I'm going to add to the problem. I'll be suggesting that you do a little more towards your exams earlier than you might otherwise have done. It's linked with the idea of taking control to build confidence and guarantee success. But I'm going to help you cope more effectively with the workload so that, overall, you won't be any worse off timewise. The extra effort from the outset will certainly reduce some of the last-minute cramming and panic. More importantly, you'll feel much more positive about the whole situation, so you'll do better as a result.

The exams are closer than you think!

At most, the academic year lasts 9–10 months. This can seem to pass fairly quickly with the result that exams begin looming much sooner than you thought. With the increasing incidence of modular exams students can be facing their first exams within 10 weeks of the beginning of the course.

The problems

Typically the views expressed by students are:

- 'I'll start thinking about the exams as we approach the end of the course. I'm certainly not going to worry about them yet, I'll only get depressed if I do.'

- 'I have far too many calls on my time to do well in exams. I just lurch from crisis to crisis, deadline to deadline and I can't seem to do anything properly.'

- 'No one has the time to do justice to the mock exams and we'll all do better when the real thing comes around.'

◆ 'I expect my teacher/tutor to prepare me properly for the exam by covering the right things and setting suitable assignments and mock exams.'

We're going to talk about making all of this easier but this means you need to start thinking about the exams right from the start. And this applies equally to whether they are 10 weeks or 10 months away. You'll see how this makes it much easier in the long run and you'll do much better than you would otherwise have done.

START THINKING ABOUT THE EXAMS AT THE START OF THE COURSE

Don't view the exams as a separate exercise
It's no good thinking about the course itself as a separate element from the exams.

> From the outset of the course you must think continually about the final exams.

By this I certainly don't mean that you should give yourself a regular shot of anxiety or depression about the dreaded final test to spur yourself on. What I am suggesting is that you keep an eye on how what you have studied today might fit into an exam question. This is particularly important for the modular exams looming within 10 weeks, but is also essential practice for the exams some 10 months hence.

For example, an economics student today (early 21st century) would recognise the topicality of the single European currency and pay particular attention to the various viewpoints being promoted in the media.

Linking the course to potential exam questions

Course topics which appear to be open to differing viewpoints are good subjects for questions which ask you to 'Discuss the advantages and disadvantages of...' So make sure you:

◆ Identify and explore these now.

◆ Ask your tutors to highlight the main points as they see them.

◆ Make brief notes for later revision and discuss them with your fellow students to share ideas.

It's the ideas and arguments which are likely to earn you the marks in an exam, and you'll get many more talking to others than thinking about it alone.

Remember the exam is not a memory test, so don't slavishly absorb the course content without thinking how it might present itself in an exam question. And the best time to think about it is as you study each element. We'll come back to this in Chapter 5 when we talk about revision generally.

The value of past exam papers

Get some past exam papers and see what type of questions come up. Familiarise yourself with the format of the exam paper and look for any patterns. Use them to get an idea of how your current studies may translate into typical questions.

We'll be talking below and in Chapter 5 about practising past papers. So get hold of as many as you can as soon as you can, and if they come with model answers so much the better.

PLANNING YOUR TIME

Life would be boring if we planned everything and only did the things we scheduled exactly in line with our intentions. Spontaneity and surprise can add much-needed excitement to our everyday existence. Unfortunately, where exams are concerned it really is vital that you plan properly. Spontaneity and surprise soon become panic and stress if you don't and you must avoid these at all costs.

So what should you be planning for?

I'm going to talk about two main areas:

◆ planning for the exam itself

and

◆ planning to fit your studying and revision into your lifestyle generally.

Start thinking about all the things that you'll need to do for the exam. In particular:

◆ Getting past exam papers and practising questions under exam conditions.

◆ Completing coursework assignments.

- Setting aside time for revision.

- Dealing with the mock exams.

Whilst we're on the subject of mock exams you must revise seriously for them. And the time spent doing this will make your final revision much easier and quicker to complete.

> Mock exams are a golden opportunity for rehearsing
> the real thing and you'll gain a lot from the experience.

We'll cover more about revision in Chapter 5.

Setting out your plans

When you've gathered all this information you will need to begin drafting an outline plan covering the period from now until the examination. Highlight the deadlines for coursework assignments as well as dates for both the mock exams and the real exams. Plan the revision periods for both. These dates are, of course, immovable so you will have to plan other commitments around them. You may then wish provisionally to allocate periods to the tasks for which you have more discretion, e.g. practising exam questions.

All of this now needs looking at alongside your other commitments in life such as:

- Coursework deadlines *which must not be overlooked.* It's very important to stay on top of these.

- Holidays.

◆ Christmas.

◆ Birthdays and anniversaries.

◆ Busy periods relating to any full or part-time jobs.

◆ Important dates for leisure pursuits, and social events.

◆ Even repainting the garden fence!

And your outline plan should now include these. *You may have to make a few decisions on priorities*. For example, a weekend away with the tennis club may not be a good idea just before an exam and a late-night celebration before an exam is also not recommended. Similarly, repainting the garden fence can wait a few weeks, whereas revising for the exam can't.

Fortunately, exams won't be with you all your life so a few sacrifices now are likely to prove worthwhile in the longer term.

Don't over-commit yourself.
Be prepared to say 'No' if asked to take on extra commitments.
Don't make life unnecessarily difficult for yourself.

Friends, family and employers are likely to be sympathetic if you explain that you have some critical dates relating to your studies which conflict with other activities.

The whole point is to *get a clear idea of your commitments* between now and the exam dates, thereby highlighting where time constraints could cause difficulties for you. You can then establish priorities and plan your time to avoid unpleasant surprises or having to do an impossible amount in a short time. In this way, you will minimise stress and avoid the situation where you don't have time to do any of the conflicting things well.

You may wish to supplement this plan with more detailed plans covering the next month or even the coming week. The degree of detailed planning required depends very much on what will work for you.

Many students find it useful, within an overall plan, to set aside a little time at the weekend to plan for the coming week. They set targets for each day and review progress against this as they go through the week. Of course the best-laid plans can go wrong, often for valid reasons. But you'll feel much more in control if you know why they've gone wrong and, more importantly, what you can do to redress the situation.

One of the great things about planning is that you can, *and must*, build in time for yourself, i.e. social or leisure pursuits or even time to watch your favourite soap episodes on TV.

View these breaks as a reward for the work you do and don't ever feel guilty about taking them. Provided they are planned carefully and sensibly within your overall commitments, you have every right to enjoy them and forget about your studies and exams for a little while.

COVERING THE SYLLABUS

In Chapter 1 we discussed taking responsibility for your own success. Making sure you cover the syllabus is a key element of this. It bears repeating here that *the day of the exam is one heck of a time to discover you haven't covered the syllabus*! So remember to:

- Get a copy of the syllabus.

- Ask the tutor if he/she expects to cover everything.

- Monitor your progress throughout the course to see whether you're covering everything.

- If not, try to establish the level of risk.

- Ensure you read appropriate course materials yourself to cover the gap.

ORGANISING YOUR STUDIES

We've discussed getting yourself organised in terms of thinking about the exams, planning your time and ensuring you cover the syllabus. Now we move on to how you need to organise your studies relating to the course itself.

Note taking and note making

Note *taking* is simply recording the more factual content of the course. Note *making* covers your analysis and interpretation of these facts, possibly in conjunction with other material. The difference is important in relation to the point I made earlier that *applying* course concepts will earn you marks rather than regurgitating facts.

Where your lectures or lessons are the key source of information you may need to take extensive notes, but where the course is well supported by textbooks or other materials then you may find the time is better spent listening and thinking about what is being said.

> What you must do at some stage, though, is make notes on the key ideas arising from the basic course content.

It's probably best done after the lecture unless your tutor offers some useful insights which you need to record at the time. In any event you should still make some more notes afterwards as you reflect on the day's teaching, either alone or with colleagues.

Organising your notes and other course materials

Part of ensuring that your final revision is as painless but effective as possible is having well-organised course materials. As well as your own notes you're likely to have a lot of other material comprising:

- Course text
- Summary key points
- Notes on potential questions
- Past exam papers
- Marked coursework
- Press articles
- Magazine articles.

You cannot afford to be confronted with a mass of disorganised papers just when you need to start your final preparations for the exam. Apart from being daunting and unlikely to make you feel positive about the whole thing, this would mean that your revision would take much longer than it needs to.

Organise your course materials from Day 1 of the course.

Fortunately there's not a lot to say about how to do this but that doesn't make it any less important. The way you keep your materials is very much a matter of personal preference and knowing what will work for you.

Loose-leaf files tend to be better than bound notebooks because you can add material later, thereby keeping everything relating to one topic together.

Some students make very few notes but tend to use a highlight marker on printed course material. Of course this can only be done if the materials are your own, it can't be done in school textbooks.

You'll need to decide whether any notes you make are clear and tidy enough to be used for final revision. Rewriting can be time consuming but it does help consolidate your learning. Consolidation can also be achieved by reviewing your notes and highlighting or summarising key points for subsequent revision.

I know some students who type up all their written notes onto a PC each week. This is time consuming but they feel that the investment of time is worthwhile.

Some students prefer diagrams or mind maps as a way of recording information, and that's absolutely fine. It's really a matter of personal choice and what works best for you.

Whatever method of record keeping and summarising you choose, the aim should be to minimise the effort needed for final revision.

A place to study

Again, no hard and fast rules other than what works best for you. But it's important to be aware of the need to establish what does actually work best. Some students feel it is important to have a place where they can work regularly with everything to hand - books, computer etc. and spread out all of their course materials without fear of disruption. The familiarity associated with this place also gets them quickly into the right frame of mind for studying. The school or college library may fit the bill if it's difficult to get this at home. Others like to relax in an armchair or on a bed, particularly for reading. Some also take advantage of daily bus and train journeys to study as well as lunch breaks etc. throughout the day. All I can say is look at all the options, decide which suit you and make best use of both the time and facilities available.

FURTHER HELP AND INFORMATION

You need to find out all that you can about the exam you're going to take. We've already discussed getting past exam papers and model answers and your tutor is obviously a useful source of information but certainly not the only one:

◆ Talk to people who have already passed the exam (they'll be quite flattered to be approached). Ask if there are any particular points to look out for. You never know what they might have found out themselves. You may even find that some of them know an examiner for the subject who will have given them some valuable pointers.

◆ Practise answering questions under exam conditions. You'll often find that your tutors will issue an open offer to mark any practice questions which students care to attempt. It's also fairly common for students not to bother unless the essay is a set requirement of the course. Talk about looking a gift horse in the mouth!

> One of the most valuable things you can do in preparing for an exam is to practise past questions and then get some constructive feedback from someone who knows the subject. This helps hone your essay technique as well as preparing you for planning and answering questions in a limited time.

◆ Get some Examiners' Reports for past sittings of the exam. Your tutor will probably have seen them or at least will know how to get hold of them. Apart from the usual comments on *students not managing their time effectively* and *not addressing the precise requirements of the question* (see Chapter 2), you may find that they'll also include commentaries on technical issues relevant to the particular subject.

◆ Where course materials seem a little sketchy or you need some more information, don't forget that libraries and the Internet are invaluable sources.

◆ Discuss the course generally or each lecture specifically with your course colleagues and ascertain the key points as well as sorting out any queries you may have. Between you, there probably isn't any technical issue that you can't resolve. Nurture these relationships and support each other. We'll cover this in more detail in Chapter 4.

LOOKING AFTER YOURSELF

In Chapter 7 we'll be talking about staying healthy during revision and in the lead up to the exam. This applies also to your whole period of study so have a quick look at that section now or at least bear this in mind when you reach that part of the book.

MAINTAINING A POSITIVE ATTITUDE

> You have every right to be optimistic and the more you get yourself organised the more confident you should feel.

You can take control of the whole process rather than let it control you!

Positive thinking

Staying positive is often much easier said than done, so here are a few tips which may help:

* Remind yourself of the grand conspiracy in your favour (Chapter 1) – everyone wants you to succeed.

* Reflect on your strengths and why you're doing the course – you probably wouldn't be doing it if you didn't have what it takes.

* Don't be too hard on yourself – get a life outside your studies and don't feel guilty about it!

* Remind yourself that you are taking control of the whole thing and you now have the recipe for success. It's all down to your own effort and technique. And the techniques in this book account for at least 50% of your chances for success.

◆ Tell yourself that you cannot afford to let nagging doubts get the better of you. This would endanger your otherwise excellent chances of success.

CHECKLIST

✓   Plan the key requirements, commitments and milestones for the period from now until the exam. Deal with any hot spots.

✓   Consider everything you learn in the context of a possible exam question.

✓   Organise all your materials and notes from the start of the course.

✓   Sort out where and when to study in a way that suits you best.

✓   Identify and use all the sources of help available to you.

✓   Stay positive and remember that you're the best person to look after your own interests.

The Role of Parents, Partners and Fellow Students

At certain times during your studies you are likely to need the support of loved ones and fellow students as well as possibly some additional help from your tutor. In this chapter we'll explore how this might be best achieved as well as acknowledging the need to reciprocate.

Even though you'll feel much better about exams when you've finished this book, you're still likely to need some further reassurance, support and practical help as you work through your studies, revision and the exams themselves. I recommend strongly that you re-read selected chapters as necessary and in particular, Chapter 8 just before the exam. But you're also likely to need support and reassurance from your family, friends, course colleagues and tutors. This applies particularly if you find that things start to worry you, that you are struggling to keep up or if issues in your private life are affecting your chances of success. Your tutor will almost certainly be sympathetic as well as able to offer useful advice. This chapter looks at the important role that all of these can play.

PARENTS
For students encountering their first taste of examinations, parents have an important role. Teenagers are prone to many pressures in

life for which parental understanding, tolerance and support are vital. The spectre of examinations is no exception and parents can play an invaluable role in helping to convey and reinforce the messages in this book. Of course this means that they have to read it themselves first and I recommend this strongly. In many instances they will have bought it for the student and that's a good start. This section is aimed primarily at them so if they haven't yet read it, ask them to do so.

Reinforcing the messages

It doesn't just end with buying the book, reading it and endorsing its contents.

Even the most enlightened student can suffer a crisis of confidence at any time, particularly just before the exams, and parents will need to reassure them gently of the key messages conveyed here.

I have certainly found this necessary with my own children even as far as the final year of university. In particular, reminding them of the techniques in Chapter 8 can help their confidence as the exams draw near.

A little coaching and encouragement throughout the year can help a great deal. Helping the students with their planning and fitting holiday and social commitments around critical times will be invaluable. Making sure that they take breaks and organising a place to study are also practical ways in which parents can ease the burden.

Reinforcing the messages on positive thinking and taking control of the process will also help, as will making sure that diet and lifestyle are conducive to good performance (see Chapter 7).

Demonstrations of support and care such as this can do a lot to relieve stress and maintain confidence and, in my experience, students respond well to this. It takes very little effort but can make a big difference. Remember, though, there is a difference between support and nagging (and teenagers are certainly very sensitive to the latter!) so bear this in mind and don't overdo it.

Bribery and inducements

Some parents offer their children material or cash rewards for success in examinations. I'm sure this achieves the required result in some cases, but I feel it does nothing for the longer term aim which I believe is to encourage them to take responsibility for their own personal development. My feeling is that support and encouragement of the non-material kind is much more appropriate.

Helping with self-development

It's worth noting for parents and students alike that from the age of about sixteen you cannot expect to be spoon-fed by teachers. In fact it's a very risky strategy to rely on this (as you saw in Chapter 1). The ideas and tips also explained there will stand you in good stead for all forms of Further and Higher Education. Parents can help students here by ensuring they are familiar with the syllabus and getting hold of past papers.

Students will certainly have to look out for themselves at university and parents can be a great help in this without being over-protective. Support and encouragement for students to deal with the issues themselves will help them a great deal in learning to cope with the responsibilities of life generally.

Helping students keep a sense of perspective

Parents should be careful to avoid comparisons of their children with others. Not everyone can achieve 'A'-grades in everything. Where students show commitment this should be praised irrespective of the results and in most cases even modest successes are worthy of praise and celebration. Expectations should be matched as closely as possible to abilities and children should also be valued for other aspects of their nature unrelated to academic ability.

Whilst very important, exam success is not the most critical aspect of anyone's life, and certainly not worth the ill-effects on health that sometimes arise. Parents should look out for the common signs of stress (e.g. difficulty in sleeping, loss of appetite, stomach upsets, etc.) and provide support as appropriate. Parents who stay calm themselves during such difficulties will help moderate the student's anxiety, but if symptoms become extreme then medical help should be sought.

Often, just listening to someone and letting them talk about their worries can be all that's needed to make them feel better. A sympathetic ear can often help someone regain a sense of perspective very quickly.

PARTNERS, OTHER FAMILY MEMBERS AND FRIENDS

Many of the points above also apply to others who are close to students. In particular, listening to their concerns and offering gentle encouragement will be very appropriate and helpful. They need to understand a student's commitments as well as sharing in the process of planning holidays, social activities, etc. in a way that supports any study requirements.

Support is a two-way process and students should try, wherever possible, to return the favour in any areas where those close to them may require help, either now or at some future date.

FELLOW STUDENTS

There are two main areas where students can provide valuable support for each other.

- Firstly, there is the moral and emotional support and reassurance needed when things appear to be getting on top of you.

- Secondly, there is a much more practical way which relates to exchanging views and ideas on the course content to improve your *understanding*. This can be achieved by setting up a *study group*, sometimes referred to as a *self-help group*.

Support and reassurance

This is similar to what we talked about above in relation to parents, partners, friends, etc. But an added dimension, where course colleagues are concerned, is that they can probably understand the problems a little better because they are subject to the same course requirements. Again the emphasis should be on *mutual* support and understanding. Many long-term friendships will begin with students supporting each other in the face of common adversity.

Self-help groups

Many students these days are finding that setting up self-help groups really increases their understanding of the course, with pleasing results at exam time. Even a brief review and chat amongst yourselves in a small group will:

◆ Help achieve a common understanding of the key points.

◆ Enable you to share ideas about potential exam questions.

◆ Give those who didn't understand any particular points a chance to get clarification from the others.

But there's also another great advantage. Constructive discussions like this can help build confidence for everyone taking part.

Share your thoughts on both the key points and potential questions with course colleagues. This is best done in a group of 2 to 4 students. Coffee and lunch breaks can be a useful time to do this or you may wish to formalise the arrangements with regular evening sessions. I know that this is yet another task I'm lumbering you with, but you can view it as a social event which may also help you to feel better about it. In fact the sessions can be split into work and social elements to maintain balance.

Choosing the right people

Not everyone is comfortable with group work and the less confident among you must not allow yourselves to feel intimidated by the more confident course participants. But it's very important that you share your thoughts with at least one other student. So choose carefully exactly whom you wish to work with.

The aim must be mutual support and benefit for all participants. This means that everyone should prepare in advance for the session and it's important for all those involved to contribute.

You should not allow a situation to develop where these sessions become a vehicle for the more gifted to show off or for the more vociferous to hog the proceedings. Equally don't let a situation develop where the less industrious simply suck ideas from the more conscientious members whilst giving nothing in return.

Co-operation not competition

Co-operation rather than *competition* is a fundamental requirement to make these groups work. You're not in competition with each other and the benefits of mutual support are likely far to exceed potential gains to be made from keeping bright ideas to yourself.

Sharing non-technical ideas

Group members can also share:

♦ Ideas for relaxation and managing stress.

♦ Techniques and tips such as those included in this book.

♦ Any relevant experiences of how they solved problems in the past which other group members are now facing.

You will find that sessions such as these are a very powerful tool in building both your technical knowledge and your ability to deal with life's problems generally. Students away from home at university usually find that they have to look to each other for support and what I'm suggesting here is merely an extension of that.

Listening

All group members should be conscious of the need to *listen*. It will be very important for those with a particular worry to feel that the others are listening. Give the talker time to make their point and encourage them with nods and smiles *without interrupting*.

> Listening should not take the form of waiting for your chance to speak – a common mistake for many.

You may then need to seek clarification of any issues and summarise the problem to show that you have listened and understood.

Flexibility

One of the great things about self-help groups is that you can operate them in a way that suits you best. You can agree the numbers, how much time you wish to spend together and how far you will take the arrangement. You can also maintain contact by telephone or e-mail if issues arise outside the meetings or if it proves difficult to get together as often as you'd like to.

Conduct of meetings

Depending on the numbers involved, the length of sessions and the frequency of meetings, you may need to introduce a little formality to make them work well. Someone may have to take the lead in organising and chairing the meetings, although you can agree to rotate this responsibility.

The agenda should be agreed either in advance or at the beginning of each meeting, to reflect as far as possible what people expect to get out of that particular session.

The chairperson should be responsible for managing the agenda within any time constraints as well as ensuring that everyone contributes and gets a chance to speak. Incidentally, all of this helps develop useful skills for later life, a useful by-product in terms of both technique and confidence. Group members should be prepared to respect the chairperson's role and not resent any instructions given by him or her to run the meeting effectively.

Self-help groups at exam time

We'll be discussing revision later and self-help groups can work really well during the final stages. Of course you will be hard pressed with your final revision but some time at least with your colleagues can really help in:

- ◆ Clarifying any queries arising from individuals' revision activities

- ◆ Providing mutual support at what can be a stressful time

- ◆ Providing a well-earned semi-social break.

CHECKLIST

✓ Recognise that you are likely to need some moral and emotional support and identify the sources available to you. Be prepared to reciprocate.

✓ Ensure that, if appropriate, your parents are familiar with the contents of this book and that they share the need to maintain a sense of perspective even when the going gets tough.

✓ Understand and share the need to take responsibility for your own development.

✓ Establish a small self-help group for the regular exchange of ideas and problems.

5

Revision

In this chapter you'll see that there is so much more to revision than the dreaded last-minute cramming session. There are less tedious and more effective ways to prepare yourself for success.

EVEN MORE MYTHS AND MISCONCEPTIONS

Having dispelled some myths about exams I'm now going to dispel a few about revision. Most students view revision as something that has to be left until the end of the course and which involves a long, boring slog through the course materials with the sole aim of memorising the content. Well, fortunately, that's not the best way to ensure success and it needn't be that boring or painful. There's a much better way; an approach that will provide a much better focus on what you must do to be successful, as well as relieving some of the tedium.

In Chapter 3 we've discussed the need to think continually about the final exams. This means thinking about how what you studied today might manifest itself in an examination question. We'll be developing this idea further in this chapter to show how it fits into an overall strategy for revision which will:

◆ Prepare you much better to demonstrate an understanding of the course concepts.

◆ Ease the final revision burden by spreading the workload and making the whole process less boring.

Some try to minimise the amount of work to be done by looking for trends in past exam papers, guessing what is likely to come up, then revising only those topics. *That's far too risky* if you're serious about success.

The problems and misconceptions

Typical comments from students relating to revision are:

◆ 'I don't mind all the coursework but revision really kills me. It's just a long, boring read through my notes in the hope that I can memorise enough to impress the examiner.'

◆ 'I have to leave revision until the last minute because if I start too early I'll forget everything.'

◆ 'Revision is all the more difficult because of the sheer volume of notes, press cuttings and magazine articles that I accumulate throughout the course and which must be sorted out before I can begin memorising everything.'

◆ 'I feel very isolated when I'm cramming and if I suddenly find I don't understand something it may be too late to get some help.'

It certainly needn't be like this and we'll now look at ways to make the whole process easier, more effective and more enjoyable.

ACTIVE REVISION

We've seen already that exams are not a test of memory but rather a test of *understanding*. So it follows that your whole approach to revision should be geared towards demonstrating your understanding of the course. You do need to remember the main points in order to apply this understanding, but the prime focus should not be on memorising. There may be some things that you are required to remember, for example, scientific or mathematical formulae and you should commit these to memory as well as having a last look close to the exam. But these are not what revision is all about.

Approach your revision in a way that is geared to understanding and constructive criticism of course topics.
This will help you remember everything you need.

We've also seen that you will not be required to *'Write all you know about...'* a subject. The danger in viewing revision as a task of memorising is that you will have prepared yourself primarily to regurgitate facts. A prime objective of this book is to prevent you from doing that.

Right from the start you must think of revision as preparation to provide clear, focussed answers to exactly what the examiner asks.

This means that you must be able to understand the various viewpoints or aspects of a particular topic in order to develop reasoned responses to questions aimed at testing that understanding. You need to develop this approach, something I call 'active revision', so that it becomes almost second nature throughout the course. In this way you will reduce the time needed for final revision as well as being much better equipped to provide suitable answers.

Active revision involves looking for and understanding the key points and arguments associated with each topic *as you progress through the course*, and thinking how these may manifest themselves in exam questions. We touched on this in Chapter 3 where we discussed the need to think continually about the exams from the outset.

Contrast this to 'passive revision' which is simply the process of memorising the facts just before the exam with no real regard for being able to do anything other than regurgitate facts.

Practising exam questions

But there's even more to it than that. *Active revision also involves practising past and potential exam questions* so that you can develop the skill to express this newly-found level of understanding in a coherent and concise manner in the time available.

This should include *some* practice of questions under exam conditions. But you don't have to go to these lengths for every question you look at. For most you will find it useful to compile an *essay plan* of the main points (alone or in your self-help group) – see Chapter 4). This is an effective technique for revision which doesn't take up too much time. We'll cover essay plans in Chapter 6. They are a key part of the revision process. They clarify your thoughts and help you assess how you could approach the question concerned.

Starting revision at the beginning of the course

You may question the value of starting revision at the beginning of the course when you've done very little and feel you'll forget anything you revise soon afterwards. However, you need to change your traditional perception of the word 'revision'. I'm talking about a different approach, which involves *thinking about everything in a wider sense* than simply absorbing facts.

Think about everything in the context
of a *potential exam question*.

This requires little effort at the time but will make your final revision much easier. It also means that you will do much better in the exams.

Students usually see the course as simply a process of taking in facts, and then they view revision as a separate, final process where these facts are memorised so that they can be replayed to the examiner. This is a very common mistake. You've already seen that the examiner doesn't want a replay of the course's factual content.

What you need to recognise is that some revision activities need to be carried out as an integral part of the course.

Don't view the coursework and revision as completely separate.
Revision is part of the learning process.

You saw above that 'active revision' means looking for and understanding the key points and arguments associated with each topic as you progress through the course, and thinking how these may manifest themselves in exam questions. It needs to become almost second nature, so you need to begin practising this as soon as you start the course. But *it doesn't require much extra effort* and the payoff at exam time will be immense.

So how do you do it? Well, it's very easy and will also make the course more interesting for you and, as you'll see below, your course colleagues.

◆ For each lecture, class or course unit (for distance learning), ensure that you have identified the important components. You're likely to have noted these down in class but the strange thing is that you don't actually learn very much simply by taking notes. Add any further information from other sources.

You need to review your notes shortly afterwards to consolidate your learning and make further notes on the main ideas.

In doing so you will have eased your final revision subconsciously by committing the details more firmly to your long-term memory. This is because the key points will have been highlighted already and you will have quickly carried out a first review of the material.

Each time you review something, it makes it easier and quicker to recall it later.

◆ Get some past exam papers early on so that, as you work through the course, you can see what sort of questions have been asked on each topic in the past.

◆ Periodically answer a past question *under exam conditions*. This is best done immediately after you've studied a particular topic to avoid the need for extensive revision. If you answer one question every few weeks you'll find it much easier to cope with the exam. Think of potential questions yourself and also answer those.

◆ For each topic ask yourself 'what might an exam question on this look like?' Some topics lend themselves more readily than others to discussion, differing views or advantages/disadvantages. So look out for these and, *after each class*, make some brief notes on the likely questions and how you would answer them.

◆ Share your thoughts on both the key points and potential questions with course colleagues (see the section on self-help groups in Chapter 7).

Predicting exam questions

Whilst we're talking about what exam questions for each topic might look like, it's worth thinking about the fairly common practice of guessing which topics are likely to come up in your exam. Students do this to minimise the amount of final revision they have to do *but it is always a risky process*. It's less risky in some cases, for example, where the structure of the exam offers a high degree of choice. But even then it's often an extensive choice *within* a whole topic or section of the syllabus meaning that you have to cover all sections of the course. Remember the aim is to build confidence through the use of *a well-planned approach* and trusting to luck doesn't support that notion.

Don't leave out large chunks of revision on the basis of a forecast or guess at what might come up.

PLANNING YOUR FINAL REVISION

You need a written revision plan

We've discussed revision activities undertaken as you go through the course, including practising past questions. We now need to think about your final revision. In Chapter 3 you saw that you need to plan some time for this. The time available will depend on your own circumstances but you must use it wisely. In most cases you'll be studying for more than one paper or subject so you must allocate the time between subjects in appropriate proportions. Plan some time for practising past questions as well as time to spend in your self-help group (see Chapters 4 and 7).

> You must produce a written revision plan.

Be sure to *plan some leisure time in your schedule*. You won't feel guilty taking planned breaks, especially if you've kept on schedule with your revision.

Finally, plan a couple of hours at the end to re-read this book or at least Chapters 1 and 8.

Revision in stages

The exams are important to you and you don't want to endure a re-sit. So I'd recommend that you set aside as much time as possible and do the revision in at least two stages:

◆ The first stage is a complete review of your notes, articles, model answers, etc. during which you may condense the key notes into a final revision summary.

◆ The second stage is a final review of these summarised points.

During these stages you should also be answering at least a few practice questions as well as just drafting essay plans for as many other questions as possible.

When to start

How early you start your *final* revision depends on your own circumstances. If you are given study leave by your school or your employer then so much the better. If not, or if this is minimal, you need to start the first stage earlier to ensure that you complete both stages in time for the exam.

Other revision activities

Any revision activities offered by your tutor should also be taken advantage of. Some students don't attend final lectures because *'it's only revision'* but these sessions are likely to be extremely useful. They usually provide valuable insights into potential questions and how to answer them as well as identifying and explaining further the more complex bits of the course. Group revision, like self-help groups, can be productive by revealing all sorts of insights and common problems.

It's a big mistake to think that time spent at final lessons is time lost from your revision schedule.

ORGANISING YOUR NOTES AND OTHER COURSE MATERIALS

In Chapter 3 we covered organising your course materials right from the beginning of the course as well as note *making* compared with note *taking*. Note making helps the revision process because it:

◆ Forces you to make sense of the topic and focusses your attention on the key points.

◆ Helps commit the ideas to memory for easier recall later on.

In addition, if you undertake the activities suggested above as you go through the course then you will have brief or highlighted notes about the whole syllabus and these will be easier to revise quickly at the end. You'll make your final revision less painful and boring in this way.

The format of revision notes

The format in which you condense your notes can be whatever you feel most comfortable with. I have seen the following used successfully:

◆ Index cards.

◆ Single sheet summaries.

◆ Post-it notes stuck on a bedroom wall.

So do whatever suits you best.

CHECKLIST

✓   After studying a topic, spend a little time *understanding* the implications of the facts and what a potential exam question might be.

✓   Regard revision as an integral, ongoing part of the course.

✓   Practise past papers under examination conditions.

✓   Organise your notes and other course materials as you obtain them.

✓   Plan your final revision carefully and include some time with your study group.

6

Special Techniques

In this chapter we're going to look at some special skills and techniques that you need to develop. You'll see how you should plan and write essays, write reports and how to deal with short-answer questions.

PLANNING AND WRITING ESSAYS

How often have you heard someone say '...she's worked really hard for her exams so she's bound to pass'. Sadly, this just isn't true if a student hasn't focussed their effort on the right things. I hope that you can see now that, in this context, 'the right things' are a combination of:

◆ *Learning* the course content.

◆ *Understanding* the key issues, arguments and viewpoints associated with the topic.

◆ *Thinking* about potential exam questions.

Having achieved all that, you're still left with the problem of how best to demonstrate to the examiner that you've done so. You can do this by planning and writing good essays.

> Developing the ability to write essays is every bit
> as important as learning the course content and ideas.

The ability to express yourself is very important in life. This applies to both verbal and written communications as well as to body language. So far as written exams are concerned you will be judged critically on *how* you communicate with the examiner as well as on *what* you demonstrate you have learned and understood.

It's not easy to acquire effective writing skills and much of it is down to practise and getting comments from others. But there are some basic ground rules for good essay writing which are easy to understand and, once mastered, will enable you to produce suitable exam answers. In this chapter we'll deal with these.

> Good essay technique means you can communicate clearly
> to the examiner who will then find it easy to allocate marks.

The value of past papers

I said above that practice is an important element in developing essay skills. Past papers are invaluable in this respect. Use them to apply the skills explained below for both planning and essay writing purposes.

What the examiner wants

In Chapter 2 we saw that the examiner wants you to:

◆ Answer the question.

♦ Use logical and coherent arguments, drawing on the course content and applying it sensibly and objectively.

♦ Structure and present your answer in a way that's easy to follow.

You can achieve all of this through the use of proper techniques for both planning and writing essays.

Approaching essay questions

The way in which you *structure and present your answer* is absolutely critical.

A well structured and clearly presented essay conveys exactly the sort of impression that gets the examiner on your side straight away. In fact, if he can see that your plan and structure is logical and he can easily pick out the key points, or even just the *key words*, it may well be that he won't even read the essay in detail. He'll just quickly award the marks for the key points and then move on. He will have been able to see easily and quickly that you know what you're doing so he can feel confident that he needn't waste time going though your answer with a fine-toothed comb.

> Get the examiner on your side right from the start and make it easy for him to give you marks.

The first stage in all this is, of course, reading and understanding the question. We'll talk more about this in Chapter 8 but for now, I'd like you to think about looking *very closely* at what the question asks. Chapter 2 discussed the need to identify and consider the key verb(s) in the question. This is the starting point – *identify these* and *focus your answers accordingly.*

Having read the question carefully and identified the verb(s) and other key words, you need to think about how you will tackle your answer. You'll be starting to think of the main points. These will generate further thoughts and you'll be anxious to get these down on paper.

Producing a plan

You need to pause briefly and think about how you can capture these thoughts, ideas and facts in a way that ensures you will produce a clear, logical and well structured answer. By all means get your thoughts down on paper *but don't start writing your answer immediately.* Jot your thoughts and ideas down in the form of a plan.

You cannot write a good essay without planning it first.

A plan will help you to:

- Collect your thoughts.

- Sort your ideas into a logical sequence.

- Structure your answer sensibly.

- View the answer as a whole and ensure it works towards a logical conclusion.

- Avoid repetition.

◆ Include all the key points.

◆ Provide a constant point of reference as you write your answer to keep you on track.

Having constructed a plan thoughtfully you will be much more able to write fluently.

If you don't have a plan then you will write things randomly as they occur to you. The result will be an uncoordinated mess which will be difficult for the examiner to mark.

A plan also saves you time by giving you a clear structure to follow. You are bound to produce a much better essay as a result.

◆ Your plan can take the form of brief notes or a diagram (mind map).

◆ Make sure that the plan addresses exactly what is required. Refer to the key words in the question. If the question asks for 'advantages and disadvantages' then your plan should include these headings.

◆ Plan the *order* of the paragraphs in a way that develops the answer in a coherent fashion.

◆ Plan each paragraph showing the main points to be covered.

◆ Leave spaces to add things that occur as you clarify your thoughts.

♦ Refer to it regularly whilst writing your answer to make sure that you stay on track.

♦ Tick off each element of the plan as you cover it in the essay to ensure that you don't miss anything out.

Essay structure

So far as *structure* is concerned there will be three main parts:

♦ *The introduction*   A brief outline commenting on the topic and showing that you have understood the question. But don't indicate any conclusions at this stage. Include any assumptions or interpretations you have made regarding the question.

♦ *The main body*   Contains the key course concepts as they relate to the question. Most of the marks will be awarded for this section.

♦ *The conclusion*   Sums up and answers the question. It doesn't have to side with any particular argument if the facts are not overwhelming and it can refer to other factors or further information that may be relevant. If you are asked specifically to express an opinion then ensure it's supported by logical argument.

The main body *must* be split into paragraphs and you'll probably find that the introduction and conclusion will require more than just one. So start thinking about what you need to say.

Consider carefully how your answer will lead from the
initial question to the final conclusion. Think about how
the arguments will develop logically and, therefore,
what each paragraph will include.

Whilst sketching out your plan refer back regularly to the question
and ensure that you are going to:

◆ Answer the question, *not simply write all you know about a topic.*

◆ Draw on relevant course material. This is what examiners expect,
what they can evaluate and *what they will award marks for.*
Introducing relevant material from outside the course can be
useful to add meaning but the bulk of your answer must be
directly related to the syllabus.

◆ Show that you have *understood* the issues associated with the
course and that you can express them in your own words.

◆ Construct a clear logical argument. There needs to be coherent
progression of ideas and arguments, a *thread* if you like, running
through your answer.

◆ Present a conclusion that looks back over the main body and
effectively answers the question. Remember, this doesn't mean
that you have to take one side or the other in a particular
argument unless specifically asked to do so (and even then you
must acknowledge opposing views).

*In fact you need to be very careful about taking sides – you run the
risk of appearing unnecessarily biased.*

- In particular, any political views must be avoided. Comments like 'the current government have made a complete mess of managing the economy' will almost certainly lose you marks. For one thing this would show that you're not being completely objective. And for another, there's always the risk that the examiner is a lifelong supporter of the current administration.

- Where you don't reach a clear view be prepared to say that the arguments are inconclusive or that there are merits on either side dependent on circumstances. What is important is to show is that you have *understood the key arguments on each side*. That is what will earn you the marks.

> The examiner is looking for an objective analysis and reasoned arguments based on your understanding of the course content and associated ideas.

Presenting your answer clearly and meaningfully

You've now gathered your thoughts and written an outline plan. You now need to craft a clear and easy-to-read answer.

Your writing style should be simple and direct:

- Use simple words, e.g. 'start' not 'commencement', 'use' not 'utilise'.

- Don't use several words where one will do, e.g. 'Now' not 'At this point in time', 'because' not 'due to the fact that'.

- Keep sentences short, i.e. 10–20 words maximum.

◆ Use active verbs not passive ones, e.g. 'The committee agreed that' not 'It was agreed by the committee'.

All of this will make it easier for the examiner to read and understand. And that's what you want.

We've already discussed dividing the essay into three main sections. And within each section your answer must be split into *paragraphs*. Many students write one continuous piece of prose. This is very difficult to read, even more difficult to make sense of and hard to mark. *The examiner will not appreciate this.*

Paragraphs should be short and cover *one* main idea. Don't be concerned about having too many paragraphs. Provided the content is relevant, the division into paragraphs makes it easier to read. It may help if you view each paragraph as a mini-essay:

◆ The first sentence should explain explicitly the main idea of that paragraph, e.g. 'Hitler underestimated the difficulties in achieving his plan to invade Britain'.

◆ The paragraph should then *elaborate* on the various reasons relating to that idea.

◆ It should conclude with a brief evaluation of the main theme.

Leave a couple of extra lines between paragraphs in case you need to go back and add something later.

As well as being short, each *sentence* should contain *one point*. These points should follow logically from one sentence to the next, developing the argument in your essay.

Punctuation and grammar are also important. But I'm only talking about being able to get the basics right. If you don't think you're as good as you ought to be in these areas you may find it useful to get a brief guide. Most large bookshops stock these and they can be incredibly useful and take only a short time to read. As well as creating a bad impression and making your answer difficult to read, incorrect punctuation and grammar can actually change the sense of what you're trying to say.

The likely effects of bad *spelling* are a little more difficult to be sure about. You shouldn't lose marks for incorrect spelling but there is always the danger of creating a bad impression. The way to deal with it is to ensure that all other aspects of your essay style are up to scratch.

> An examiner would find it very difficult to condemn a well structured, well argued and clearly presented essay if all that was wrong with it was poor spelling.

WRITING REPORTS

Many of the points made above in relation to essays apply to questions asking for a report e.g.:

◆ Ensure that you read the question carefully to determine precisely what is required.

- Plan your answer and pay attention to the structure.

- Draw on the course material and ideas.

- Construct logical arguments.

- Adopt a simple and direct style.

There are also some additional features of report writing that you need to be aware of which will earn easy marks.

Your plan can take the form of brief notes or a diagram (mind map).

The most basic of these is that if a question asks you write a report then that is exactly what you must do!

This sounds obvious but students regularly write an essay where a report is asked for. This is usually another example of not reading the question properly, which will lose you marks unnecessarily.

Specific formats

If the course is one that may require a report to be written in an exam, then it's likely that your tutor will have talked about the type of format which is appropriate to the subject. For example, a science subject may require a fairly rigid format showing the method adopted, equipment used, an examination of potential errors, etc. But for more general subjects the following rules are likely to apply.

The heading

The report must be clearly headed showing:

- The addressee, e.g. 'Report to The Managing Director'.
- The author, e.g. 'From Mike Evans'.
- The subject.
- The date.

These are all very simple and items which will earn marks, but so often omitted.

The introduction

This is similar to that for an essay, i.e. a brief introduction to show that you have understood the topic. Include any assumptions you have made in interpreting the question. Don't be afraid to use a little creativity to make it look realistic. For example, if the question asks you to write a report to your Managing Director on the implications of re-siting your head office to a local business park, then you may wish to open it with 'At our recent meeting you asked for a report on...'. But don't get too carried away with this sort of thing at the expense of time spent on the key issues.

The main body

This is where you apply the ideas from the course as for essay answers but geared more to presentation of:

- the method used in any investigations
- analysis of key issues and evidence
- main findings.

Conclusions and recommendations

Most reports will require some conclusions and recommendations. These should be objective and refer to the need for further investigation where the facts may be inconclusive. The idea is to show an objective analysis of the subject matter drawing on the course concepts.

It may also be appropriate to show any risks or sensitivities associated with any proposed course of action.

SHORT ANSWER QUESTIONS

Not all examinations require essays or reports. Many require short answers on specific topics. These are regularly found in maths and science questions which are designed to test your understanding and knowledge of basic course concepts. The answer is less likely to require a plan and a carefully structured essay, but layout and style will still be important. Even short answers must be clear, concise and logical. Again, avoid long sentences.

> Short answer questions still require very careful reading
> to determine exactly what is required.

This is particularly important for maths and science questions where the requirements can be very exacting.

Mathematics question will require answers to be laid out clearly showing the method adopted and all the calculations. This is particularly important because if you make an error in calculation, you will still earn marks for the *method* adopted, which is likely to be more important than actually getting the correct answer. If workings are not shown or are unclear then the examiner will be unable to see the reasons for an incorrect answer.

Where answers are capable of prediction within a certain range, which is often the case for maths and science, then it will be important to show that your answer has been evaluated against this. Always show the units where appropriate e.g. 1220 *metres*, 800 *km/hour*, 500 *volts*.

Where diagrams or tables are required then pay attention to layout. The aim should be to make them clear and easy to read, so use sufficient space and always label them with *units* used, e.g. gms/cc, kms/hour, etc.

CHECKLIST

✓ Always read the question carefully whatever the type of exam.

✓ Make sure you can demonstrate a clear *understanding* of the key issues, arguments and viewpoints associated with each course topic.

✓ Take a little time to *plan* both the content and structure of your answer.

✓ Pay particular attention to the *layout* and *style* of your answer.

✓ Where the questions asks for a report pay particular attention to the recommended *format*.

✓ For short answer questions adopt a clear concise style, paying particular attention to methods and units used where appropriate.

As the Exam Approaches

This chapter deals with important issues in the run-up to the exam. This is when all the irrational fears and myths are likely to surface again and even if you've taken on board the lessons in the preceding chapters, your newly-found confidence may still be under threat.

We're going to look at:

◆　Maintaining confidence and control.
◆　Reminding yourself what the exam is about.
◆　Using your final revision time effectively.
◆　Looking after yourself.

You've now disregarded the common myths about exams and taken control of the whole process. You've planned your study and revision time and gained a clear understanding of the syllabus as well as the likely *types* of question. The month or so leading up to the exam is a critical time because you must do the things which will ensure that you walk into the exam room feeling confident.

IT NEEDN'T BE AS PAINFUL AS YOU THINK

But it doesn't have to be too painful. Of course you will have a lot of revision to cover, but a marathon read through of everything is not the way to succeed. You need to plan your revision, vary the workload a bit and share thoughts with some carefully chosen course colleagues. You must also plan your revision in such a way that you revise at a time of day that suits you best, and most importantly, in a way that gives you some time off, even in the last few days.

Stay positive and in control.
Use your time wisely and don't be too hard on yourself.

THE COMMON PROBLEMS

Typical views on the final stages are:

+ 'The last month is the worst. The pressure builds up and I find it difficult to cope with all the work.'

+ 'Final revision has to be about cramming during every spare hour that I have.'

+ 'I've got more than one exam to do and I just don't know how to plan my revision.'

+ 'During the last couple of weeks I get really miserable because I can't do anything except revise. And if I try to give myself a break I feel really guilty.'

+ 'I need coffee and comfort foods during revision to keep me alert. This, as well as worrying about the exams, means I don't sleep very well.'

MAINTAINING CONFIDENCE AND CONTROL

Dismiss negative thoughts

You've seen how you can take control of the process and you've planned your approach like a well executed military campaign. But as you get closer to the exam those nagging doubts and long-held feelings about exams start to surface again. Well there's a simple answer to this – *don't let them!*

Each time a negative thought enters your head about the exam, replace it with a positive one.

You can find plenty of reasons to be positive in this book, so keep it to hand and refer to it if you start to get a little anxious. Remind yourself that no one is trying to catch you out, that everyone wants you to pass (including the examiner) and that success is all down to your effort and technique. Have another look at Chapter 1 and remind yourself of the grand conspiracy going on in your favour, not against you.

You can't afford to let nagging doubts get the better of you. This would endanger your otherwise excellent chances of success.

Stay in control of the situation

Remember that the techniques explained here account for *at least 50% of your chances for success*. The other 50% is down to the work you have to do in covering the course work and revision activities. That's the harder bit and takes up a fair amount of time over the academic year. Reading and understanding this book is the easy bit, but is just as important. The really good thing is that you can read it in a couple of hours, so why not read it all again in the run up to the exam? Seriously though, as a minimum, *you must read Chapter 8 just before each exam*, it contains absolutely essential and invaluable advice.

> Stay in control of the situation,
> don't let the situation control you.

I've talked about working with other, carefully selected people and I'll be saying a little more about this on pages 87–88. But there can also be a very negative, destructive effect from taking too much notice of others. You can start to presume that they're cleverer than you are and that they've done much more work than you have. Then your confidence takes a knock and you start to become anxious again. Some of this is due to the loud braggarts, we've all come across them, but they're few and far between and are best avoided. Remember also that your reaction to others' posturing is your own responsibility and you can choose to ignore them.

> But mostly these fears aren't a result of others' actions,
> they're all in your own head.

Tell yourself:

◆ I am in control and I can cope.

◆ I've done everything possible to ensure that I will pass.

◆ Other people's actions are irrelevant to my success. I work in a way that suits me.

◆ I will plan my revision carefully and I can get it done in time.

◆ Unlike most candidates, I now have the techniques for success.

Think about your strengths and recognise the progress made so far.

Exams are easy

If you're one of those individuals who think that 'I always do badly in exams', well, you needn't think that any more.

> Exams are not a problem for those who have approached the course with the right attitude and techniques.

Exams have become a problem through myth, irrationality and as something to blame by those who haven't worked and therefore, don't deserve to pass. In fact, by the time you enter the exam room the worst is over, all the hard work has been done and you now have 2 or 3 hours to show how well you can do. This will pass very quickly and, in all probability, fairly painlessly, so it's unlikely to be an ordeal.

REMINDING YOURSELF WHAT THE EXAM IS ABOUT

A test of understanding

Remember it's not a memory test. The exam aims to test your *understanding* of the course topics and ideas. So it's important in the last few weeks to bear this in mind and *plan your revision* including some time to:

- Review your notes of potential questions.

- Practise some essays under exam conditions (don't forget to write a plan for each as part of your practice).

- For as many other questions as you can, compile a brief essay plan for each to see how you would answer it.

- Think about essay technique and the things you learned in Chapter 5. In particular, remind yourself of the need to write concise, legible, well structured answers that will *make it easy for the examiner to allocate marks*.

The structure and requirements of the exam

Make sure you understand the *structure* and requirements of the exam paper in advance:

- How many questions you will be required to answer.

- Whether questions sometimes have options within them.

- Whether some questions are compulsory.

- Whether the paper is divided into parts with a requirement to answer questions from each.

- How long the exam lasts, and how to allocate your time (see Chapter 8).

- What books and materials you will be allowed to take into the exam room.

- The marking scheme – do some questions carry more marks than others?

But don't think that this lets you off the need to read the instructions very carefully on the day itself, there's always the chance that next time may be different.

USING YOUR FINAL REVISION TIME EFFECTIVELY

A multi-stage approach

We discussed active revision and revising in stages in Chapter 5, so by the time the exam draws near you've already made some revision notes of the main points. You need to read through *your entire course material* well in advance of the exam date. At that stage you may wish to edit your revision notes (or compile them if you haven't previously done so) to provide something that can be reviewed more quickly at final revision stage.

Some students even summarise their revision notes further to a level at which they can review briefly the main concepts in a few hours on the day before the exam. How far you go in this respect is really up to you. But what is important is that you don't expect to revise all of your notes and coursework in one marathon reading session very close to the exam.

This multi-stage approach doesn't just mean that you end up with a nice set of revision notes. There is another great advantage. Having had more than one review of your notes you will have consolidated your learning very effectively and this alone will help you to:

◆ Recall facts more easily.

◆ Get through your final revision more quickly.

Active revision and summarising notes
eases the final workload and helps your memory.

Planning your final revision

Your final revision needs to be carried out *as close as possible to the exam date*. The techniques referred to above will certainly help you to achieve this, but you will need to compile carefully a *written final revision timetable* as follows:

◆ Determine the time available. Ideally you need some study leave from school, college or work. Those at work may wish to supplement this with some holiday entitlement (it's probably worth the investment in the longer term).

◆ Note any unavoidable commitments.

◆ Build some free time into your schedule for relaxation etc., and *don't feel guilty about it* (see 'Looking after yourself' below).

◆ Divide the remaining time between the various subjects.

Self-help groups

Spending a little time revising with your self-help group can be very productive. This involves all parties having read the appropriate material and then discussing the key points and likely exam questions. The advantages are:

- It breaks the monotony and isolation of revising alone.

- Students can learn a great deal through hearing the views of others. This often sparks off ideas that neither party had previously thought about.

- It provides valuable moral support at a time when there is a danger of anxiety rearing its head again.

- It helps promote the process of *understanding* rather than simply *revising* facts.

Remember though, the emphasis must be on *equal contributions* by all involved, so everyone must come to the sessions well prepared. Your time is valuable at this stage, so these meetings must be made to work well. An ideal number for such a group is you plus one to three others and you should meet regularly for say, an hour or so.

> Plan your revision carefully and maintain at least
> some contact with carefully selected course colleagues.

LOOKING AFTER YOURSELF

You cannot afford to neglect yourself in terms of mind, body and spirit. You're probably feeling a little anxious as the exam approaches and you have a lot to do. You may find that you neglect some of the important things in your life such as:

- Your social life.

- Relaxation and leisure time.

- Time with your family and friends.

- Exercise.

- A healthy diet.

Your aim must be to arrive at the exam in as good a physical and mental state as possible. So don't tire yourself out with work and don't wear yourself out with the wrong type of lifestyle.

Time out

Of course your free time will be restricted but *you must have some time for yourself*. So plan some breaks into your schedule. If you have study leave so that whole days are allocated to revision, then don't expect to work all day. Somewhere between five and seven hours solid revision is all most people can expect to do. And if you achieve this level of work then you can feel very pleased with yourself. A useful approach is to:

- Find the time of day that suits you best for studying. For me it's very early morning, but some people work better late at night.

- Plan your revision time during these periods and, equally important, plan time off during the rest of the day.

For me, working first and rewarding myself with time off afterwards was a successful approach. Whilst on study leave, I worked from 7.00a.m. until around 4.00p.m. *with coffee, lunch and tea breaks.* I then had every evening free. I knew that I was incapable of absorbing information for more than 5–7 hours, so I didn't let myself feel guilty for having the rest of the time off. I have known this strategy work well for many people. It requires discipline but you can have planned breaks and view them as *a reward for hard work*.

If you don't have much time for final revision, for example, if you are in employment and forced to revise in the evenings and at weekends then it's not so easy. But the basic principle still applies. You must plan breaks into the schedule.

Diet and exercise

Also pay careful attention to your diet and exercise. Healthy eating and drinking and short walks or even strenuous exercise will help your mental state and you'll revise more effectively.

During those last few weeks avoid late nights or excessive alcohol intake but maintain at least some sort of social life.

Many students tend to overdose on coffee, tea and chocolate. This gives short bursts of energy but it doesn't last and it interferes with blood sugar levels. As a result they get slumps in mood and concentration. Sipping water regularly and snacking on fruit is likely to be much better in terms of maintaining your energy levels.

Sleep

During the period leading up to the exams, get into a routine before going to bed. Try to unwind and avoid coffee, soft drinks and chocolate. Play music, read a book or do anything else that relaxes you.

The day before the exam

All of this becomes even more critical in the last day or two before the exam.

◆ Don't burn the midnight oil on the night before the exam. You should be skimming through revision notes only. I suggest that by 7 p.m. at the latest you should close your books and tell yourself 'That's it, all the hard work is over, all I need to do now is think about my exam technique'. This is covered in Chapter 8 and at this stage is the only reading you should do.

◆ Check you have everything you need in terms of pens, pencils, rulers, calculators, spare batteries (or ideally, a spare calculator) etc., for the following day. It's a good idea to compile a written checklist well in advance.

◆ Recheck the time of the exam. I have known instances where students turned up in the afternoon for an exam held in the morning!

◆ Have a relaxing evening and go to bed early enough to get a good night's sleep.

◆ Don't plan to do any revision on the morning of the exam. It's too late, and tends to create feelings of panic.

◆ If you're not familiar with the location then check out train and bus times in advance. If you're driving make sure you know whether you'll have any traffic jams to deal with and where you can park. You may even wish to make a practice journey to ensure that traffic queues won't be prohibitive or that your chosen car park doesn't regularly fill up before you get there. Make sure you have contingency plans to cover delays or cancellations of public transport, unforeseen traffic problems, etc.

◆ Avoid last-minute contact and conversation with other students. Strike a deal with your revision colleagues that, even if you meet on the morning of the exam, you will not discuss it. It won't help any of you and some of you will start to panic because you will think (probably wrongly) that others have done more work than you.

◆ Allow yourself to feel a little nervous on the day, it'll get the adrenaline flowing and bring out the best in you.

Aim to arrive at the exam calm, collected, refreshed and cautiously optimistic.

CHECKLIST

✓ Don't allow anxiety to take over now, get rid of negative thoughts and stay in control.

✓ Remember that the exam will test your understanding and application of the course.

✓ Plan your final revision carefully and stick to your plan.

✓ Pay particular attention to your physical and mental health.

✓ Think about the practicalities of getting to the exam venue.

8

The Exam

In this chapter we look at the big day itself. We've already discussed changing your attitude and building confidence and you've seen how important it is to read questions carefully and plan answers. All that remains now is for you to learn some very simple but amazingly effective techniques to use in the exam room.

THE IMPORTANCE OF EXAM TECHNIQUE

Failure through poor exam technique is very common, even for hard working, clever students. But the good news is that the types of mistake are also very common and are easily avoided. We'll now look at:

- Staying cool, confident, calm and relaxed.

- Reading the exam paper and selecting the right questions.

- Managing your time.

- Reading the question.

- Answering the question.

- What to do after the exam.

Techniques for dealing with the exam are at least as important as being well prepared through revision.

A tutor from a very well known business school was once heard to remark that, with proper technique, you can achieve a pass in any exam without knowing anything about the subject! – an exaggeration perhaps, but the point is very well made.

Ironically, the effort needed to master these techniques is minimal but the results can be quite amazing. The techniques are easy to understand and apply and they can be referred to quickly and easily as a last-minute reminder.

Students who have covered the course subject matter and a suitable amount of revision have already done the hard bit. Using the techniques outlined in this chapter they can virtually guarantee success. Those who have not worked so hard on the course or revision may well also find that the use of the proper techniques will partly compensate for a lack of knowledge and provide them with a pleasant surprise when the results are received!

THE COMMON PROBLEMS

Typical views of exams include:

◆ 'I get really keyed up just before an exam and, all of a sudden, I think I won't be able to remember anything.'

◆ 'I like to read the exam paper quickly and get stuck into the first question as soon as I've got a rough idea of what's required. I get really worried seeing other people well underway when I've not started.'

◆ 'I always run out of time so I think a good approach is to answer fewer questions than required but do them really well.'

◆ 'I hate finding out after the exam that I misunderstood a question. But I usually console myself that I've written enough to show the examiner that I know all about the subject really.'

All of this can be easily avoided.

STAYING COOL, CONFIDENT, CALM AND RELAXED

Maintaining a healthy perspective

By now you should be feeling pretty positive. In Chapter 1 you saw how to get a perspective on the whole exam process. You now understand what examiners want and you know how to get them on your side and make it easy for them to award marks. And in the last chapter you saw that the worst is over because all the hard work has been done. But it's only natural to feel a little apprehensive, and that's fine as long as this is supported by an underlying feeling of quiet confidence.

> A little nervous tension can bring out
> the best in you during the exam.

◆ If panic starts to set in go somewhere quiet and take a few deep breaths.

- Smile to yourself – it will help.

- Don't do any last minute revision – other than reading this chapter.

Don't allow any negative thoughts to take hold. Replace them immediately with positive ones. Remember what you learned in Chapter 7 and tell yourself:

- I am in control and I can cope.

- I've done everything possible to ensure that I will pass.

- Other people's actions are irrelevant to my success. I work in a way that suits me.

- Unlike most candidates, I now have the techniques for success.

Think about your strengths and recognise the progress made so far.

A crisis of memory?

It's fairly common for students to think at this stage that they can't remember anything and that their mind has gone blank. This sometimes prompts a frantic last-minute read-through of revision notes. This does nothing to help your performance, it puts you in completely the wrong frame of mind and, as we'll see, is completely unnecessary.

It happened to me on virtually every occasion, but each time I found that exam questions prompt sufficient recall as I began to focus on the answer. In fact I found that I usually recalled too much, and knowing what to leave out was more of a problem than remembering enough to put in. Most students find this to be the case.

Don't reach for your notes for some last-minute skimming to prompt your recall. You will remember things as you start to read the questions and plan your answers.

Memory for exams is developed through active revision:

◆ Making sense of the key ideas.

◆ Understanding the course concepts rather than trying to learn them by rote.

◆ Multi-stage revision.

One very successful student I knew made the effort, on the day of each exam, to clear his head as far as possible and not think at all about what he had revised. He found that this helped him to recall what was needed as he approached each question.

On the day
Try to do everything without having to rush:

◆ Check you have everything you need before you set off, e.g. writing materials, calculators, money for fares, etc.

◆ Arrive early and use the time to take a short walk.

◆ Don't be tempted to take a last minute glance at your revision notes.

◆ Avoid contact with other candidates as far as possible. If you must travel with or meet friends then agree in advance not to talk about anything related the exam (see Chapter 7). This may be difficult to achieve but someone is bound to be displaying symptoms of stress and, unfortunately, *anxiety can be infectious*. So do whatever you can to avoid contact with such people.

◆ If you arrive late, most examining boards will allow you to enter the examination room up to 30 minutes after the start of the exam. In such cases don't panic (it won't help), just work within the reduced time available, managing your time accordingly *to attempt all questions* you are required to complete. It will be even more important than usual to attempt the full number if you are to maximise your chances of retrieving the situation. You'll just have to do shorter answers but still write your essay plans.

Illness

Hay fever can be a particular problem at exam time and for this, or any other problems on the day, it may be worth checking in advance what arrangements exist for informing the exam board. The invigilator or your school/college may have appropriate forms for you to complete, allowing the exam board to consider any individual circumstances.

READING THE PAPER AND SELECTING THE RIGHT QUESTIONS

Ignoring others

The people in the room who began writing within 30 seconds of getting the paper are well on the way to failure. But you should be ignoring everyone else anyway.

> Other candidates' writing speed and requests for extra paper
> are totally irrelevant to your chances for success.

This is a very important learning point. Students, in a heightened state of tension, tend to judge their actions closely against others more than ever. You must avoid this at all costs – it will do you no good whatsoever.

Stay calm while you read the question paper

Stay calm, keep up the slow, deep breathing or anything else that works for you and spend about five minutes reading the instructions and all the questions.

> Don't hunt frantically for the first topic that looks
> vaguely familiar and start your first answer.

♦ Read the instructions at the top so you know how many questions you have to answer.

♦ Then read each question carefully to ensure you can answer everything it specifically asks for.

♦ Turn over the paper to ensure you've not missed out any questions on the back (it happens!)

♦ Recheck the instructions for how many you need to select.

♦ Begin the selection process.

The selection process

Remember, it's extremely unlikely that you will be asked to 'Write all you know about...'.

So don't select a question solely on the basis of the subject content. You saw in Chapter 2 how to ascertain *exactly* what you are required to do. Look for words like:

- analyse

- assess

- compare

- describe

- explain

- discuss

- illustrate

- list

...*and make sure you can,* for the subject involved.

The *format* will also be important, for example, if the question asks for a report then you will lose marks if you write an essay. If you're asked to provide examples or diagrams then you must do so.

You will be judged critically on whether you have done what you were asked to do.

Once you've selected your questions, answer your best one first.
This will boost your confidence.

Multiple choice questions

Many students underestimate multiple-choice exams. They feel that
it's easier to select a correct answer from a given list than having to
think up your own. And if you don't know the answer then you can
guess. The problem with all of this is that they are often designed so
that more than one option may be close to the correct answer and
this can create confusion. Also the chances of guessing the right one
are usually 1 in 5 and some multiple-choice exams actually deduct
marks for wrong answers.

They require an equally disciplined approach. In particular:

- Read the instructions carefully and underline key words in the
  questions as you get to them.

- Check the *sense* of the question. Look out for negatives and
  double negatives.

- Be sure to read *all* the answers provided, don't stop when you find
  one that you think is correct.

- Look out for answers that are almost identical.

- Don't even think about doing minimal work and guessing
  randomly. *The odds are not in your favour.*

> Don't underestimate multiple-choice exams,
> they are every bit as testing as written ones.

Many students adopt a special approach for multiple choice questions which you might like to consider. They mentally answer the question without looking at any of the choices listed. They then look for the answer that corresponds to their own, not having been led by confusing wording. But they still read *all* of the answers given – some can be worded very closely.

MANAGING YOUR TIME

Answer the required number of questions
The examination paper is put together very carefully and sufficient time is allowed to complete it. The intention is that you should complete it and furthermore you are *instructed* to answer a specific number of questions.

> The strategy of answering fewer questions
> but doing them 'really well' is seriously flawed.

Not only have you ignored the carefully considered instructions, but you are also seriously reducing your chances of success. Assuming 20 marks per question, a student who answers 4 questions rather than 5 immediately limits the maximum marks obtainable to 80%. If the pass mark is 50% then he must achieve an average of 62.5% over 4 questions. This is much more difficult to achieve than 50% per question. It's as simple as that.

The way to avoid the problem is also very simple.

Allocate your time proportionately and
spend no more than the allotted time on each question.

Dividing up your time

If the examination is 3 hours long and the required number of
questions give 100 marks, then you have 180 minutes to gain a
maximum of 100 marks. This allows 1.8 minutes per mark, so for a
20-mark question you should allow 20 times 1.8 minutes, giving 36
minutes. You may decide to allow yourself 31 minutes to plan and
write your answer with 5 minutes reading time at the end. Similarly,
for a 10-mark question in a 3-hour paper you should allow a total of
18 minutes. In a 2-hour paper this would be 12 minutes (1.2 minutes
per mark).

Monitoring your time

You must monitor your time carefully throughout each question and
aim to finish it on time. As you reach the final few minutes, wind up
your essay. You can leave some space on your answer sheet to return
if you find time later.

After spending the allotted time on a question, leave it and move
on immediately to the next – whatever stage you have reached in
your answer.

Many students find great difficulty in moving on from a question
before they have finished, but it is vital that you do. Apart from the

need to maximise your potential marks, the points to be gained in the final few minutes are likely to be considerably less than those gained in the opening few minutes of the next question. So you may spend an extra 10 minutes (that you don't have) in chasing 1 or 2 marks as opposed to gaining 7 or 8 on the next question.

Provided you have revised sufficiently there is absolutely no excuse for answering less than the required number of questions.

Managing time for multiple-choice questions

The rules are the same for multiple-choice questions. Allocate your time proportionately and move on after the allotted time. The time available for each question will of course be small, but you must avoid the tendency to get bogged down on any one question. If you're struggling with a question don't guess at the answer. Move on and come back to it at the end. If you're still unsure, then just give it your best shot.

READING THE QUESTION

Re-reading carefully

You've already read the question at selection stage but before beginning your answer you must re-read it and:

◆ underline or highlight key words

◆ identify any separate components.

Consider the question:

'Outline the events leading to the outbreak of the Second World War. Comment on the assertion that Britain could have avoided declaring war on Germany.'

The words 'Outline', 'Second' and 'Comment' are critical and should be highlighted. Also note that there are two distinct parts to the question and the marking scheme will reflect this. The answer must be divided into two parts, not amalgamated into a single narrative. *This is the start of your essay planning process.*

For questions split into the format (a), (b), (c) it is easier to identify the component parts, but these should still be scrutinised for key words.

> Read the question again before you begin your answer.
> You should have read it carefully at least three times before you start.

Examiners' reports repeatedly comment that students have not read the questions properly. Tension, panic and the desire to 'get stuck in' are often the cause, but you can't afford to risk such a fundamental mistake. Having spent months on a course of study and revision it's little short of tragic to fail for the sake of a few minutes composing yourself and going through the simple steps outlined above.

Maths and science questions

These require extremely careful reading because of the innate requirements for accuracy in copying mathematical or scientific expressions. If you misinterpret or copy down an expression with incorrect positive or minus signs, or with parentheses in the wrong place, or with the wrong unit of measurement, then the whole sense of the question will be changed. Often answers are designed to work out nicely, so carelessness resulting in a wrong answer may mean you waste valuable time looking for the error.

ANSWERING THE QUESTION

A clear and well-focussed answer

Having read the question and understood exactly what's required you are now well placed to write a clear and well-focussed answer.

Remember, your aim is to make the answer easy for the examiner to read and understand, and therefore, easy for him to award marks in accordance with his predetermined scheme. This applies equally to essays, reports and short-answer questions.

Essay plans

A word of warning. For essay-type answers, students regularly lose that clear focus and drift off into irrelevancies. So how do you avoid this? It's easy – remember from Chapter 6 that:

You must construct a brief essay plan.

This will take up more valuable time. But it will save you more time by giving you a clear structure to follow. You are bound to construct a better essay as a result.

◆ This will impress the examiner and help clarify your approach.

- Your plan can take the form of brief notes or a diagram (mind map).

- Give your plan a heading (i.e. 'Question 3 Plan') and hand it in with your answer.

- Make sure that the plan addresses exactly what is required. Refer to the key words in the question. If the question asks for 'advantages and disadvantages' then your plan should include these headings.

- Plan each paragraph showing the main points to be covered.

- Leave spaces to add things that occur as you clarify your thoughts.

- Refer to it regularly whilst writing your answer so that you stay on track.

- Tick off each element of the plan as you cover it in the essay to ensure that you don't miss anything out.

- Avoid 'padding out' your answer with irrelevant material. Everything you write must have a clear relevance to the question.

Remember that you must maintain a clear focus on what has been asked for. Don't lapse into 'write all you know about. . .' mode. This will not impress the examiner. It'll just make it more difficult for him to allocate marks.

And don't waste time writing out the question at the beginning of your answer.

AFTER THE EXAM

Avoid post mortems

When the invigilator tells you that the time is up he might as well add,'...you are now free to leave and undermine each other's confidence', because this is exactly what happens. Candidates leave the room and immediately begin comparing how they approached certain questions, what they included, what they assumed was asked for, etc. Those who found it difficult will be unnerved even more by others who say they found it straightforward or easy.

> This is all completely pointless.

In this situation, as in life generally, there is nothing to be gained from worrying about something over which you have no control.

In any event, no one can get everything absolutely right each time and you can afford to get some things wrong (see below). You will inevitably find in post-exam discussions that some students will have included things that you didn't and vice versa. And in your heightened state of tension you're all likely to overreact to even the smallest omission, so:

- If your exams are over, simply forget about them and await the result.

- If you have other papers to take, concentrate on those. Getting depressed about the previous one will serve only to affect your chances adversely.

♦ Avoid those people who insist on going over the details.

It's best to agree with your colleagues in advance that you will not enter into post-mortems. Otherwise, simply leave the building on your own after the exam and forget about it!

I was once absolutely convinced I'd failed an examination. I had found it difficult whilst several of my colleagues commented that they'd found it easy. I began studying for a retake and even bought additional textbooks. I didn't wait at home for the postman on the day that the results were due. I had in fact passed.

Even if you think you've done badly, you may well get a pleasant surprise, especially if you've followed the advice given in this chapter.

Learn from the experience

No matter how well you prepared for the exam and used the right techniques on the day, there are likely to be some things that you wish, with hindsight, that you'd done differently. Don't let this depress you. Remember, you can't expect to get everything right. In fact you can get quite a few things wrong and still pass. A grade 'A' requires between 70% and 80% depending on the exam, so you can lose quite a lot of marks and still achieve an excellent result. So don't worry about the odd thing, or few things, that you think you got wrong.

View these things as learning points. Turn them into a positive result and learn from them for the future. Many people will be taking exams for many years, so you can expect to get better at them as you get older.

CHECKLIST

✓ Allow yourself a little nervous tension but, equally, ensure an underlying feeling of quiet confidence.

✓ Read the instructions and questions carefully. Make sure you know how many questions you need to do. Highlight key words to determine exactly what each question is asking for.

✓ Allocate your time to ensure that you will complete the examination. Move on as soon as the allotted time is up for each question.

✓ Read each question carefully before answering, highlight key words and identify all component parts.

✓ Plan your answer and refer to the plan regularly as you write.

✓ Avoid post-mortems.

✓ Learn from the whole experience.

Index

Quick Solutions to Common Errors in English
An A–Z guide to spelling, punctuation and grammar
Angela Burt

'You will never doubt your written English again.' – *Evening Standard*

'A straightforward and accessible handbook for anyone who ever has a query about correct English – and that's all of us.' – *Freelance News*

'This is an excellent book; good value and useful ... buy it!' – *V. Tilbury, Cranfield University*

ISBN 978-1-84528-361-2

Writing a Report
How to prepare, write and present effective reports
John Bowden

'What is special about the text is that it is more than just how to 'write reports'; it gives that extra really powerful information that can, and often does, make a difference. It is by far the most informative text covering report writing that I have seen ... This book would be a valuable resource to any practising manager. ' – *Training Journal*

'With the help of this sensible step-by-step guide, anybody can develop first-rate report writing skills.' – *Building Engineer*

ISBN 978-1-84528-293-6

Model Everyday Letters
How to write and set out formal letters and documents
Angela Burt

'...from writing a formal acceptance of a wedding invitation, putting together a job application letter and saying the right thing in an absence note for a child who has been away from school There are correct and incorrect ways of this kind of everyday writing, and Angela Burt shows just how it should be done.' – *Writers' News*

'...so helpful in guiding you through the formalities and principles.' – *Writing Magazine*

ISBN 978-1-84528-316-2

Improve Your Punctuation and Grammar
Marion Field

'Invaluable guide...after reading this book, you will never again find yourself using a comma instead of a semi-colon.' – *Evening Standard*

'I can't recommend this book highly enough. Every writer should have a copy.' – *Writers' Bulletin*

ISBN 978-1-84528-329-2

How To Write Essays
Don Shiach

'Guides to essay writing enter a crowded field but this one has the merit of being concise and clear and its advice plainly comes from someone with a lot of practical experience of teaching writing. As someone who teaches students to write essays I would have no hesitation in recommending this title. It is attractively written and laid out and it will be of immediate value to anyone who wants to master the art of essay-writing.' – Amazon

ISBN 978-1-84528-341-4

Introduction to Research Methods
Dr Catherine Dawson

'I would certainly recommend this book to others. I found it extremely informative and will refer to it often.' A reader, UK

'It is compact, practical, easy to read and well laid out. If every student kept a copy by him/her during the course of the research, as a quick guide, it would certainly assist methodology and results.' – *Training Journal*

ISBN 978-1-84528-367-4

Read Faster, Recall More
Use proven techniques for speed reading and maximum recall
Gordon Wainwright

In today's information laden world, time is valuable. Reports, reference books, contracts, correspondence, newspapers, magazines and journals are just some of the things you might need to read and digest on a daily basis.

If you feel that the speed at which you read these items and the extent to which you are able to retain their information could be improved, then the use of the practical tips, proven techniques and numerous practise exercises in this book could help you to reach your potential. With the aid of this invaluable book, you can save time and achieve more.

'. . . will help you to reduce the time spent on reading and recalling information.' – *Evening Standard*

'. . . purely practical and aims to help you in the professional environment.' – *The Times*

'A worthwhile investment.' – *The Guardian*

ISBN 978-1-84528-162-5

Writing an Essay
Brendan Hennessy

This lively and practical guide takes you through the whole process. With it you'll write essays of distinction every time.

'There's a lot of good sense in this book.' – *Times Educational Supplement*

'If you're a student, buy it.' – *Writer's Monthly*

ISBN 978-1-84528-249-3

Writing Your Dissertation
Derek Swetnam

'I wish I had read this book before I had started to write my dissertation. The chapters are relevant and helpful and contain information such as some of the most common spelling mistakes. This book is a great basic start.' – *Amazon Reader Review*

'This book has been a lifesaver! Half way through a dissertation I suddenly realised that I was drifting aimlessly. This book gave me guidance and helped me to structure my dissertation plan when I needed it most. I would definitely recommend it to others!' – *Amazon Reader Review*

ISBN 978-1-85703-662-6

Touch Typing in Ten Hours
Ann Dobson

With this book you can learn to 'touch type' in ten hours at a *fraction of the cost* of a course. It will also take you *less time* than the average course and, best of all, *you can learn in your own home or office*. Just think how much time you will save in your working day – and you will be able to concentrate on the content rather than finding the correct letters. *Touch Type in Ten Hours* contains easy-to-use lessons divided into manageable one hour blocks, and there are plenty of exercises to consolidate what you have learned. There is also a reference guide giving useful 'tips of the trade'.

ISBN 978-1-84528-340-7

How To Books are available through all good bookshops, or you can order direct from us through Grantham Book Services.

Tel: +44 (0)1476 541080
Fax: +44 (0)1476 541061
Email: orders@gbs.tbs-ltd.co.uk

Or via our website
www.howtobooks.co.uk

To order via any of these methods please quote the title(s) of the book(s) and your credit card number together with its expiry date.

For further information about our books and catalogue, please contact:
How To Books
Spring Hill House
Spring Hill Road
Begbroke
Oxford OX5 1RX

Visit our website at
www.howtobooks.co.uk

Or you can contact us by email at info@howtobooks.co.uk